ANDREAS GRYPHIUS

HERR PETER SQUENT~

ANDREAS GRYPHIUS

HERR PETER SQUENTZ

Edited
with Introduction and Commentary
by
HUGH POWELL
Head of the Department of German in the
University of Leicester

LEICESTER
UNIVERSITY PRESS
1969

First published in 1957 by Leicester University Press
Second edition 1969

Distributed in North America by
Humanities Press Inc., New York

Copyright © P. H. Powell 1957

Printed in Great Britain by Lowe & Brydone (Printers) Ltd

SBN 7185 1089 5

To
RUDOLF MAJUT
SCHOLAR AND GENTLEMAN

FOREWORD

GERMAN literature is notoriously deficient in great comedy. The reasons for this are complex, and although much has been written on the subject, little notice has been taken of the comedies of the seventeenth century. It is astonishing that the first important author of comedy in the German language, Andreas Gryphius, has been almost completely neglected as such in this country. *Peter Squentz* is the only light play by Gryphius that has been printed here, and on that occasion (fifty years ago) it was bowdlerised for use in schools. It is hoped the present edition will do something towards repairing this deficiency. The text reproduced is from the 1663 edition of Gryph's works, i.e. the last supervised by the poet himself. The play, which is based on an adaptation of an episode in *A Midsummer Night's Dream*, is of interest to social historians as well as to students of literature and the theatre; and this by virtue of its burlesque on itinerant actors and pseudo-scholars, as well as the references to Hans Sachs and the Master-singers. It informs us, moreover, of the sense of the comic which animated an educated audience in seventeenth-century Germany.

My aim has been to clarify the place of this little droll in the main-stream of German comedy, such as it is; to relate it to the life and out-look of Germans at the time in which it was written; to explain allu-sions and linguistic obscurities which have been hitherto disregarded; and to render possible a keener appreciation of the comedy than is likely to emerge from the study of a plain text. The book as a whole is a companion volume to my edition of *Carolus Stuardus*, and includes no study of the poet's life and Weltanschauung, nor of his works other than the comedies; this is to be found in my Introduction to *Carolus Stuardus*.

Peter Squentz is eminently performable, and it may not be a forlorn hope that, apart from being studied as a text, it will be produced on some of our university stages. It is in a performance that the play is fully savoured.

I gladly acknowledge my debt to my colleagues: Dr T. W. Craik for valuable hints concerning the pre-Shakespearean drama; Mr G. C. Gray for advice on the transcription of the musical score; Dr G. B. Pyrah for showing once more great care in preparing the manuscript for the press; Dr Kurt Wölfel, at present Lektor in the German Department of the University College of Leicester, for several helpful suggestions; and the Library Staff of the College, especially Miss Joanna Hatfield, for their co-operation and courtesy. Once again the encouragement and patience shown by my Wife have been of inestimable help to me in this project. For some years I have enjoyed the privilege of being able to draw on the vast and profound scholarship of Dr Rudolf Majut here in Leicester, and I dedicate this little book to him in respect and gratitude. Finally, I have an especial reason to be grateful to the University College of Leicester for undertaking the publication of this work.

In this second edition a slight revision of the Commentary has been made and a few misprints corrected. Some items of important recent secondary literature have been added to the Bibliography.

The University
Leicester
October, 1968

CONTENTS

ILLUSTRATION

INTRODUCTION

SOME ASPECTS OF COMEDY IN GERMANY
UP TO THE SEVENTEENTH CENTURY

It is impossible to understand the serious without the comic.
—Plato, *Laws*, vii, 816.

GENERALLY speaking the cause of laughter is the contrast between what is and what should be, the incongruity that can arise from an association of the imperfect with the ideal, of pretence with truth. This is met with, of course, in day-to-day life, and the earliest attempts to present imaginary persons and actions before an audience probably included laughable situations and incidents. The kind of laughter evoked by the man slipping on a banana skin is age-old, and moreover the life-pulse of that most ancient sort of comedy known as clowning. The incongruousness which makes us laugh is not, however, confined to physical experience. As with the progress of civilisation man developed into a more social and sophisticated being, not only was the range of his experience extended, but his responses to an increasingly complex existence became subtler. In European drama a more refined sort of comedy emerged in which social criticism was either explicit or implicit. The spectator was now not only moved to laughter, but persuaded to reflect on the moral conduct of the characters and on their relationship to each other. This intellectualised type of social comedy assumed, broadly speaking, two forms—the comedy of manners and the satire. Amongst the Ancients the two most distinguished authors of the comedy of manners were Menander and Terence; in modern times Molière and Oscar Wilde. If the attitude of these writers to the foibles of their contemporaries is tolerant and polite, the satirist is liable to be (but is not necessarily) impatient and unkind. The laughter he has in mind may be unfriendly, and through the medium of derision he can reprove because he is indignant at the waywardness of man (Brant, Jonson, Pope, Swift), or he may, in a detached way, present the folly of men with the hint of a corrective (Molière, Sachs).

Comedy in the Middle Ages was generally of the 'low' order, and buffoonery was not long finding its way into the Mysteries. As early as 1170 the Abbess of Hohenburg complained that unseemly jests and clownery were penetrating religious plays.[1] In the old Easter plays, for example, the scene in which the younger disciple John raced with Peter to the sepulchre and beat him (John xx, 4) soon developed into comedy. In one Tyrolese play John taunted Peter with having a poor physical condition caused by too much drinking.[2] While we must be careful not to assume too readily that all was comic to medieval man that seems so today, we can see unmistakable signs of a sense of fun in these passion plays.

In the minds of our ancestors of five or more centuries ago virtue was associated with wisdom, vice with folly;[3] hence in their plays the devil could appear as a comic figure, that is, of course, when they were performed outside the church. He was invested with all the traditional features—long, black, shaggy body, horns, claws, tail, and enormous eyes—the sort of creature which in the popular imagination held sway over a subterranean furnace into which he tossed all damned souls. He was amusing with his acrobatic tricks, his howls and moans (when, for instance, he learned that Hell had burnt out).

Comic effects were also produced by remote-sounding names and strange languages. These were either laughed to scorn or misinterpreted. In the Middle Ages this happened principally in the use of Latin, but since the sixteenth century modern foreign languages, and with the birth of a standard literary language in German, dialectal peculiarities became a source of amusement.[4] The shepherds in the nativity plays, for example, spoke in dialect. These shepherds, too (and here we come to another comic element in the old plays) were laughable because of the incongruity of their humble state and their privileged position at the side of the infant King of Heaven. Finally, the braggart Roman soldier at the Crucifixion in the Easter plays was not an entirely new character, but his personality obviously had the ingredients of comedy.

A. THE INTERLUDE

THE emergence of the secular play in the sixteenth and seventeenth centuries, the Shrovetide farces of Hans Sachs and others, strengthened an earlier tendency to make the peasant the scapegrace. In the old nativity play the confusion of the shepherds when the angel visited them by night, and the subsequent pilgrimage to Bethlehem

---

[1] W. Creizenach: *Geschichte des neueren Dramas*, Vol. I, p. 64.
[2] K. Holl: *Geschichte des deutschen Lustspiels*, p. 8.
[3] This was still the case in the sixteenth century, e.g. Murner's *Narrenbeschwörung* (1512) and *Grosser Lutherischer Narr* (1522). Cp. also Brant's *Narrenschiff* (1494).
[4] Cp. p. xxxix.

provided comic relief (not ridicule).[1] Such scenes were the beginning of the interlude which by the sixteenth century had become a
separate play in lighter vein, inserted between the acts of the serious
drama, or run parallel with a static scene in the drama proper. Creizenach[2] mentions a production in Zwickau in 1518 of Terence's *Eunuchus*.
The record has it that two additional plays were performed between
the acts; in the one seven women quarrelled over one man, in the other
seven peasants wooed one maiden. Sometimes interludes were introduced to hold the spectators' attention during a lengthy and unexciting
scene; for instance in Hans Salat's *Verlorener Sohn* (1537) a story is
recited during a banquet scene. This reminds us of John Heywood's
well-known interlude of the *Four P's* (1540), also played during a
banquet.

An important advance in the development of the interlude seems to
have been made when a Mecklenburg schoolmaster, Franciscus Omi-
chius, introduced into his play *Dionysius, Damon, und Pythius* (1578) an
interlude based on a scene from M. Bado's Shrovetide play in Low
German, *Der Bauer Claus*. The principal drama is about Damon and
Phintias (the story in Schiller's *Bürgschaft*) and has nothing in common
with the burlesque peasant scenes. There seem, however, to have been
technical reasons for the placing of the first and last of these, for the
first comes between the dispatch and return of a messenger, and the
last to fill a prolonged space of time in the main plot. (Claus Narr sings
whilst a meal is in progress in the major drama.) Seven years before
Omich's play Richard Edwards's 'tragical comedy' *Damon and Pithias*
appeared in England. Here, too, we have a succession of scenes, mostly
farcical, which fill in the time between Damon's departure and return.
The important difference between these comic scenes and the interlude
in Omich's play is that the former are enacted by characters in the main
drama, and are part and parcel of it.

By the end of the sixteenth century the interlude was becoming a
convention. The Brunswick pastor Melchior Neukirch tells us as much
in the foreword to his *Stephanus* (1591), adding that the purpose was to
raise a laugh. Heinrich Julius of Brunswick adopted it from the first
and showed some virtuosity in the use of different dialects. Indeed it is
these comic scenes which constitute the Duke's important contribution
to German drama, not the tragedies and tragi-comedies proper. The
Nürnberg writer Jacob Ayrer excelled the Duke in the portrayal of
human nature, and in his numerous tragedies there are more funny
situations than in any of those of his predecessors; moreover his comic

---

[1] Cp. H. Knaust's *Geburt Christi* (1541), Bartholomaeus Krüger's *Anfang und
Ende der Welt* (1580), and Georg Göbel's *Jacob* (1586).
[2] *Op. cit.*, Vol. III, p. 249.

episodes grow in importance until they become a secondary plot. The Silesian pastor Martin Böhme (Bohemus) used his native dialect for the episodic scenes and wove them into his main drama with considerable success.[1]

The popular demand for comic episodes in tragic plays early in the seventeenth century is recorded by Johann Rist,[2] who explains how his first tragedies were favourably received by connoisseurs, and goes on:

„die meisten aber waren nicht allerdings damit zufrieden allein darum / weil keine sonderliche Pickelheringspossen mit untergemengt wurden / dahero ich genötigt war / zu einer jedweden tragischen oder traurigen Handlung / derer insgemein drey / ein lustiges Zwischenspiel sonst Interscenium genannt (die gleichwol mit dem rechten Haubtwerke eigentlich nichts zu schaffen hatten) zu setzen / worauff meine Spiele alsbald ein großes Lob erlangten."[3] An interesting piece of evidence this, too, of the consideration scholar poets were beginning to give to the tastes of a broader public. Christian Weise, a little later, was demanding the inclusion of interludes instead of the division of a drama into five acts.[4] Rist owed his considerable reputation as a dramatist in the seventeenth century to the interludes and not the allegorical plays themselves. His use of the Holstein dialect may not have been always intended to appear laughable, but it was the practical outcome of a principle he himself enunciated. In his introduction to *Friedejauchzende Deutschland* (1653) he insisted that characters on stage should speak the language they would in real life; e.g. peasants did not speak High German.[5] In the preface to *Perseus* (1634) Rist disclaims any satirical intent in his interludes and declares he introduced them to please the simple folk. Andreas Gryphius tells us in the preface to *Peter Squentz* that he had arranged for the comedy to be performed publicly "nebens einem seiner Traurspiele." It may have been performed as an afterpiece instead of during the intervals between acts.

The next important stage in the development of the interlude in the seventeenth century was at the same time its climax: Gryph's *Gelibte Dornrose*. This play can and does exist independently,[6] for although written in dialect and intended for performance act by act between the

---

[1] Cp. *Schöne Comedia vom Alten und Jungen Tobia* (1618).
[2] *Aller Edelste Belustigung Kunst- und Tugendliebender Gemühter* . . . (1666), p. 121.
[3] There was to be an echo of these words over sixty years later. Cp. p. xxxvi below.
[4] Cp. Preface to *Der Grünen Jugend nothwendigen Gedancken* (1675).
[5] The English playwright Richard Edwardes had made similar demands some eighty years previously. Cp. his Prologue to *Damon and Pithias*.
[6] A full appreciation of it, however, requires that it be studied in connection with the other play, set, as this is, on a higher social and literary level.

acts of *Verlibtes Gespenste* (a *Singspiel* in High German), it is a self-contained play, being poetically a greater achievement, and revealing higher technical skill than the more dignified play it was meant to serve as accompaniment. Indeed the term 'interlude' seems inadequate when applied to a play of such quality and proportions.

B. THE FOOL

EVEN a brief survey of the growth of comedy in Germany cannot ignore the rôle of the Fool. The origin of this important figure is not known precisely. We have already seen that the devils in the old Mystery plays were sometimes comic in their appearance and behaviour, but they did not monopolise the comic element in the medieval theatre. The criers who announced the play and commanded silence for the performance were apt to amuse the crowd with their antics like the juggler and merry andrew. The Fool in the Swiss play by Josias Murer *Der jungen Mannen Spiegel* (1560) tells us:

> es iſt ein alt harꜩomner ſitt
> den lan ic neꜩ ouch gälten
> das gwonlich loufend narren mit
> in ſpꞑlen von ꞑewälten
> wiewol man ſꞑn nit wort wil han
> man ſchempt ſich unſer allen[1]

A century later Gryph's Peter Squentz introduces his own play, and is obviously regarded by his aristocratic audience as a Fool:

Theodor: . . . Was wil der alte Lappe mit dem hölꜩernen Ober=Rocken?

Eubul: Den träget er an ſtat des Zepters / weil er ſich zum Vorreder des Traur=Spiels auffgeworffen.

Seren: Es iſt kein Kinderwerck / wenn alte Leute zu Narren werden.

By the sixteenth century then, this comic figure had acquired the name of "Narr," and although he was sometimes still outside the play, i.e. appearing before and between scenes, he was recognised and accepted as a distinct personage in dramatic performances. With reference to the Shrovetide plays performed by schoolboys, Goedeke quotes[2] from

---

[1] Cp. K. Weinhold: Das Komische im altdeutschen Schauspiel (*Jhrbch. f. Litgesch.*, Vol. I, p. 32).

[2] Vol. II, p. 331.

the *Nordhäuser Schulordnung*: "Doch soll er (der Rektor) acht Tage vorher den Pastor . . . einladen, auch den Narren im Spiel hart einbinden, damit sie, weil sie personae larvatae sind, an keinem Bürger oder den Seinen Muthwillen üben."

The evolution of the identity of the Fool in drama was possibly associated with the spread of the institution of the court fool which reaches back at least as far as the twelfth century, and experienced a boom in the late fifteenth and sixteenth centuries.[1] This is, however, not to deny that the court jester with his dignity and frequently formidable talent enjoyed a different status from that of the clown with his horseplay.[2] Gradually in the sixteenth century the Fool's rôle within the German play was consolidated, but he was still not a key figure as he came to be in Shakespeare's comedies. Rather was his function to relieve the gross tedium of the morality plays. This he did in a variety of ways; he could play the buffoon, for instance in the manner of the Shrovetide plays, or as in some of Heinrich Julius' plays, he could be witty like the court jester, or he could be merely sententious and moralise with cold maxims, that is be quite unlaughable. What is certain is that in sixteenth-century German drama he had not yet become one single type.

About the middle of the sixteenth century small groups of professional actors from Italy appeared in the south of Germany. The plays they performed became known as the *commedia dell arte*—a name which seems to indicate that the exponents were specialists in their work.[3] These plays were generally written around a central character which was the zany or fool. The playwright was the leader of the troupe and generally played the chief rôle himself. They were not written out in full; instead the main situation and action were sketched out, and the dialogue improvised at the time of the performance. As the actors wore masks, emotion had to be expressed by gestures other than facial. Although the activity of the Italian players was largely confined to South Germany (especially to Bavaria), the arrival of the *commedia dell arte* was important for two reasons above others. Firstly, this was the first acquaintance the Germans had made with a foreign *professional* theatre; secondly, in these performances the part of the Fool was vital and central, rather than incidental and marginal.

It is perhaps fruitless to speculate on the probable development of the

---

[1] Pickelhäring in *Peter Squentz* is described as "des Königes lustiger Rath." In Act III Squentz, who has been the victim of a practical joke, says to the king: "Es giebet leider viel Narren auff euren Hofe."

[2] In England it was Richard Tarleton who first enjoyed the distinction of being both official court jester (to Queen Elizabeth) and a successful clown on the stage.

[3] Cp. A. Kutscher: *Die Commedia dell arte und Deutschland*.

German stage fool, had not the English itinerant players arrived on the continent towards the close of the sixteenth century. It is a fact, on the other hand, that the clown was a vital part in their repertoire also. If we try to assess the nature of the rôle of this foreign clown, we should bear in mind that, just as the plays these actors performed were garbled versions of English dramas, the clown's part was almost certainly perverted. The English players did not become famous in Germany for the poetry in their plays, but because of the sensational and comic appeal of their stage productions. They had behind them the tradition of Nicholas Udall who in the Prologue to *Ralph Roister Doister* (1541) wrote:

> Nothing more commendable for a man's recreation
> Than mirth which is used in an honest fashion.
> For mirth prolongeth life and causeth health.
> Mirth recreates our spirits and voydeth pensiveness.

Their clown was not a mere raisonneur, but also a practical joker and coarse jester. This was the sort of stage fool Jacob Ayrer became familiar with in Nürnberg at the end of the sixteenth century, and his plays brought not only a more human and humorous Fool in Johann Clam, one given less to moralising and more to lively fun, but they also constitute a landmark in the history of German drama. The old morality play with its interminable sermonising and occasional light relief now gives way to a drama, at least temporarily secularised, which brought a new idea of the comic, and with its mixture of instrumental music, songs, and dances—and atrocities—was solicitous of the applause of the audience.

C. THE ROMAN TRADITION

A STUDY of the elements of comedy in German drama up to the seventeenth century must take account of the rôle played by the comedies of Terence and Plautus.[1] The works of Terence were well known to the German scholar of the Middle Ages. Their merit as *plays*, it is true, seems not to have been noticed at the time, and they were in fact studied because the style in them was regarded as a model for students of Latin. Here, possibly, is the reason why Plautus with his linguistic obscurities was neglected. Moreover, apart from learning to write elegant Latin, the young scholar came face to face with a variety of human types such as existed in his own day.[2] The majority

[1] Cp. K. O. Conrady: Zu den deutschen Plautusübertragungen (*Euphorion*, Vol. XLVIII, pp. 373-396).

[2] Compared with Plautus and Aristophanes, Terence had, too, the enormous advantage of Donatus' commentary which had been published in Germany in 1499.

of these may have been unsavoury, but by making their acquaintance
the student was supposed to learn about the world and so fortify himself against its snares and vices. In the Middle Ages, however, the
primary function of Terence's works seems to have been linguistic, and
not until the sixteenth century when translatioṅs of the Latin poets
abounded, were they used for moral-didactic purposes in the first place.
The period of Humanism also brought a significant extension of the
audience reached by a writer like Terence. It was no longer confined
to the student within the university or monastery walls but, with the
spread of school performances, included a wider range of people from
the middle classes some of whom had no knowledge of Latin.[1] New
editions of Terence and now Plautus, too, were provided by meɹ like
Erasmus, Melanchthon, Rollenhagen, Greff, and Albrecht von Eyb. In
1535 Greff published his translation of Plautus' *Aulularia*, and hoped
that more such comedies would be acted and read, "jn sonderheit aber
vom gemeinen man verstanden." The events and characters were still
set in ancient Rome, but spectator and pupil-player were encouraged
to see their own society mirrored in these comedies.[2] Luther himself
urged his flock to read them.[3] The conception of drama as a *speculum
vitae* became universally accepted. A new prologue or epilogue was
added to the translation in order to emphasise the moral, and this, of
course, was based in these sixteenth and seventeenth-century versions
on the Christian ethic. I think that in the performances of Terence and
Plautus at least, the comedy of situation was enjoyed by the audience,
but the plays were published and performed in the first place for the
didactic use to which they could be put. The frequent recurrence on
title pages of the phrase *kurzweilig und nützlich* (prodesse et delectare)
bears witness to this dual purpose.[4] It is probable that by about 1550
the middle-class German audience recognised certain of its own features
in the Roman plays and laughed at them. For these comedies were
about people in comfortable circumstances and the problems that beset
them, and in sixteenth-century Germany the burgher was class
conscious as never before.

---

[1] For an illustration of the manner in which Terence's plays were adapted, see
Goedeke's *Grundriß*, Vol. ii, p. 508.

[2] Cp. the English Plautine comedies *Ralph Roister Doister* and *Gammer Gurton's
Needle*.

[3] Cp. Goedeke, *op. cit.*, p. 330.

[4] Sir Thomas Eliot, the sixteenth-century scholar, had advocated the study of
Terence and Plautus for the same reason.

SOCIETY AND LITERATURE
IN SEVENTEENTH-CENTURY GERMANY

THE structure of German society in the seventeenth century is sometimes seen as a pyramid with the sovereign at the apex and the lowliest of the community, impoverished peasants, serfs, and so on representing the broad base. The figure is admissible and apt, not least of all because of the way in which the eye of the beholder is drawn from the base to the apex. But we have no need of the simile, for the pattern of society in those days is plain for all to see in the arrangement of the interior of the theatre.[1] The sovereign sat in a central position nearest the stage and at eye-level with it. Either side of him and behind him were his family, friends, and courtiers—the whole constituting the highest social level. In the first row above sat the state functionaries, on whom the reigning despot relied for the administration of his realm. The next row above accommodated the mercantile class and craftsmen, those who enjoyed court patronage being especially privileged. Still higher, just beneath the ceiling, the servant class, including those attached to the wealthy and influential members of the audience. The gaze of most in the auditorium rested in the direction of the sovereign, seated as he was just in front of the stage.

Now this structure of society was regarded generally as divinely ordained; the ruling prince was God's representative in the temporal world, and as such supreme and infallible. By and large the poor accepted their portion in life, and protested only against extreme harshness and cruelty. The monarch was after all their *Schirmherr*, and they liked to be allowed to see something of the magnificence of court ceremony, even if it was no more than a peep at an opera performance or a firework display. Such occasions led them to feel that they *belonged* to the world of their august lord. But no impoverished peasant had a right to expect advancement, should he happen to be more talented than his fellows. From the sovereign's point of view *Volk* was *Volk*, and as long as their religious needs were met, there was no further obligation to improve their lot. The prince himself, however, did have need of the hurrahs of the townsfolk which resounded in his ears as he

---

[1] Cp. W. Flemming: *Deutsche Kultur im Zeitalter des Barock* (*Handbuch der Kulturgeschichte*), p. 30, and M. Fürstenau: *Zur Geschichte der Musik und des Theaters am Hofe zu Dresden*, erster Teil, facing p. 328.

drove through the streets. He liked to bask in the warmth of their cheers and was glad of their thanks for royal bounty.

The prince was surrounded by the *Hofadel*—those members of the nobility who served their liege daily and depended largely on his grace and favour for their standard of life. The right of awarding patents of nobility was no longer the prerogative of the emperor, and virtually anyone of the rank of *Pfalzgraf* or over could bestow the coveted title. This privilege enhanced his power in his domain; he was the source of bounty not only for the courtiers and the masses, but also for the middle class, especially the professional men—writers, scholars, medicos, and so on.

The hierarchy in this aristocratic society was very finely graduated. This is still evident from the subtle distinctions in the mode of address recorded in contemporary letters and dedications in books. Each individual was highly conscious of his rank, very proud of any advancement, and it was this pride in grade and position and respect for superior status which produced the cohesion that kept the social pyramid together. Thus it was that the ready recognition of the privileged position of the nobility was associated with a serious concern on the part of the middle class for their own standards of culture and behaviour. During the previous century it was they who had produced the representative authors, poets, and artists, and although the Thirty Years' War caused some cracks and crevices in the social fabric, the professional men—clergy, teachers in school and university, and civil servants—were still a force to be reckoned with. Some of them even were content to remain commoners; Andreas Gryphius, for example, did not use the patent of nobility conferred on him as a youth by his friend and patron the Pfalzgraf von Schönborn. There was, however, a difference in the tone, the mental attitude of the middle class of the seventeenth century compared with its counterpart in the previous period. This is to be ascribed to changes in the pattern of society, and to the way in which the commoners were now drawn into the orbit of the reigning sovereign. The way of life of the burgher underwent a reorientation in the light of the new representative rôle assumed by the ruling prince, who was now the supreme arbiter of fashion. The burgher became a satellite to a degree his forbear during the golden age of the *Reichsstädte* had not been. The nearer his profession brought him to the court, the more brightly he reflected the glory of the throne.

This professional class, the most highly cultured in the whole community, owed its importance to a sound education in the Humanities, a close acquaintance with religious doctrines, a lively interest in historical, geographical, and scientific studies, and the experience accumulated by extensive travel. It was more worldly, more open to secular influences than in the previous century when the principal mentor was the pastor. In Melanchthon, the Praeceptor Germaniae, and alongside Luther the dominant figure in sixteenth century Germany, we may see a rare blend of humanism and religious zeal. During the age of absolutism, on the other hand, whenever the theologian spoke with authority he was a court functionary or university teacher as well, that is, saddled with new responsibilities additional to the spiritual guidance of his flock. Johann Rist, pastor, *Kirchenrat*, and playwright embodied the new type of scholar-official. The heyday of the pedant with his barren store of learning was past[1] and, as we shall see, he became a butt for the ridicule and satire of the seventeenth-century moralist. It is probably true to say that the scholarly section of the middle class now entered into a closer association with the ruling dynasty than at any time previously. As to their relationship with the court nobility, while differences in rank and origin continued to be observed, both social strata had in common a fund of culture and shared to some extent at least the same mental climate. Here Heinrich Julius, Duke of Brunswick and Liselotte von der Pfalz come to mind—to mention only two intellectually gifted members of ruling dynasties at the beginning and end of the century. Gryph's life-long friendship with the Kurfürstin Elisabeth is an example of the cultural bond between prince and burgher.

Since about the last quarter of the sixteenth century especially, the prince with his retinue of aristocrats set the fashion and pattern of life which were echoed in some measure all the way down the social scale. In the novels of the period (e.g. by Lohenstein and Zigler) they appear as the central figures, whether the authors are aristocrats or commoners. If we compare these with the stories of a Wickram or a Fischart, we see how the direction of interest has veered away from the middle-class sphere of life to that of the aristocrat. Nevertheless it is the humanism developed and cultivated by the middle class in the sixteenth century which constituted the nucleus of culture in the age of absolutism, and outlasted the courtly fashion dominant in the narrative of the time. The scholar-poet was probably never really at ease with the language, manners, and ideals of the *Amadis* novels, and early in the second half of the century Bucholtz the Brunswick clergyman was already endeavouring to satirise this type of literature.

The ravages of the War undermined the economic structure of the land, one consequence being the ruin of some families of the ancient nobility (they are represented in Gryph's *Horribilicribrifax*), and another the disappearance of many wealthy patrician families. Their places were filled by the heads of new commercial houses whose business

---

[1] A long time was to elapse, of course, before he disappeared entirely.

acumen had quickly made them fortunes during the period of bewilderment and bankruptcy immediately after the War. With the cessation of hostilities land became once more a secure investment and most of the new capitalists bought up whole estates. Their wealth gave them power and influence with the princes who in many cases had been reduced to straitened circumstances. They became candidates for the nobility and endeavoured to take a short cut to the manners and way of life of the aristocracy. Their efforts in this direction made them also a target for the satire of the scholar poets. On the other hand the new rich here and there furthered the cause of the arts by patronising poets, painters, sculptors, and architects, and in this way made a contribution to the cultural life of the community.

Within the Reich the peasant was ever an oppressed and exploited member of society, as indeed elsewhere in Europe, but his lot had worsened distinctly since the Peasants' War (1525). In 1555 the Augsburg Reichstag recognised serfdom as legal, and well on into the seventeenth century the notorious practice of *Bauernlegen* continued, i.e. the compulsory surrender of land to the landlord. In eastern parts the peasant had long since enjoyed less privileges as a bondsman than his counterpart in western districts. Probably under the influence of the feudal system in neighbouring Poland the peasant gave personal service to the landlord in greater measure than in the west, where his tribute tended to take the form of dues and taxes. Meanwhile during the War, utterly at the mercy of marauding soldiery at least half of which were cavalry, he suffered on the whole more than any other member of the community. For the nature of his trials we need seek no further than Grimmelshausen's *Simplicissimus*. The impecunious peasant had always been illiterate, but since the comparatively rapid spread of culture following the invention of printing had passed him by, his social position deteriorated still further. But even he did not remain entirely untouched by the influence radiating from court and ducal palace. To this day the ceremonial *Bauerntracht*, especially in the south, has retained something of the extravagance and 'over-dressed' appearance of the Baroque. . . . The peasant continued to speak his dialect as of yore, but since the introduction and acceptance of a standard literary German after Luther's translation of the Bible, the dialects were coming to be regarded in a different light by those who had received some sort of education. Thus it happened that the peasant's speech, together with his rough manners and nature which had been coarsened considerably by his experiences in the War, evoked the ridicule of a number of writers in the Germany of that time.

The vicissitudes of war, waged as it was largely with the help of mercenaries who had no sense of loyalty to one cause or another, inevitably multiplied the flotsam and jetsam of society. These displaced and dispossessed persons included the mendicant war-cripple, the lady of quality turned harlot, the depraved student, the wandering minstrel, the strolling player and acrobat, and best known of all perhaps, the discharged officer and braggart who would swindle his closest associate to satisfy an idle whim. All these again appear in Grimmelshausen's colossal panorama of war-time Germany.

For over a generation German-speaking territories had been overrun by a motley host of *soldateska*, camp followers, and other parasites from all other European countries including Britain.[1] The Reich was a veritable Babel of languages. Predominant among the foreign tongues was French, and so high was the prestige of France as the most cultured and civilised country, that all manners and types of people contrived to speak at least a smattering of it. Next to French came Spanish and Italian as fashionable foreign languages, and it was the custom for those who were very conscious of their limited education to garnish their speech with outlandish words, as the rural population does to this day in certain parts of Germany. The ignorant swaggering ex-soldier masquerading as a cultured linguist is immortalised in Gryph's Horribilicribrifax.

In the foregoing I have made occasional reference to the reflection of various characteristics of seventeenth-century German society in the literature of the period. Perhaps the most severely critical social commentary is to be found in the epigrams of the Silesian Friedrich von Logau; the most detailed in the *Gesichte* of Moscherosch who hailed from the south-west. The first was a nobleman, the second a commoner. Moscherosch was a writer of patriotic sentiment who felt very keenly both the depravity and brutalisation of his countrymen, and the loss of their national individuality as a result of the wholesale adoption of foreign customs. He wrote with anger and bitterness in his heart. Possibly he felt himself to be in a cleft stick, for his own 'visions' were in form those of the Spaniard Quevedo. Schupp, a clergyman who had broadened his education by extensive travel, found a more personal tone in which to satirise social evils. His sermons and pamphlets are distinguished by pithy language and the absence of that garrulousness so prevalent at the time. They were inspired by a sincere desire to reform the way of life of his contemporaries.

If in the satirical work mentioned so far the dominant emotion is indignation, in the Low German *Scherzgedichte* of Johann Lauremberg we find a freshness and humour which have survived three centuries. He is altogether less censorious, more tolerant of the follies practised by

[1] In our own time these have been portrayed by Bertolt Brecht in *Mutter Courage und ihre Kinder*.

his fellows—and few escaped his notice. Another man whose serious mission in life did not prevent him from using humour and wit as weapons against human vice was Abraham a Santa Clara, for many years court preacher in Vienna. The numerous plays of Christian Weise in the second half of the century also show that their author confronted stupidity and waywardness with severity and amusement. They were written, it is true, in time of peace when some of the more extreme human vices were not as prevalent as during the War. But apart from the change in circumstances there is an unmistakable shift in the attitude of the author, which strikes us for example in *Die drei ärgsten Erznarren in der ganzen Welt*. Here there is ruthless exposure of humbug, pretentiousness, and sheer dishonesty, no matter in what guise they were concealed. Quack doctors and quack professors, astrologers and soothsayers, plagiarists, braggarts, parvenus after a title—all come under scrutiny, but they are not so much scourged as ridiculed. As headmaster of a school Weise was closely concerned in the moral training of his pupils; as a scholar he was naturally interested in the world of letters. In his work, then, we are treated to burlesque, parody, and satire. In literature the elaborate style known as *Schwulst*, and Zesen's linguistic reforms are among his targets; nor did the lawlessness in the publishing world escape his attention.

In comedies like the *Bäurische Macchiavellus* we are shown the egoism, quarrelsomeness, and depravity of the peasants, but as Weise himself says of his *Liebesalliance*:

„Es ist doch ein elend jämmerlich Ding um aller Menschen Leben. Vnd wer solches in fremden Bildern vor sich sehen kann / der ist ohn' allen Zweifel nicht geärgert / sondern vielmehr zu manchem Nachdenken angeführet worden."

The audience and reader, then, are to be encouraged to lead a life based on sound ethical principles, and on an acceptance of their allotted place in society. Weise's early comedies owe much to Gryph's; there is, for example, a marked resemblance between Gryph's *Horribilicribrifax* and the *Bäurische Macchiavellus*, and between *Peter Squentz, Tobias und der Schwalbe*, and the *Zweifache Poetenzunft*; but this is another subject. For the time being it has been my purpose to show that a certain amount of social criticism was practised in literary circles in seventeenth-century Germany, and that the contemporary comedy carried its share of this criticism.

COMEDY IN SEVENTEENTH-CENTURY
GERMANY

A. THE THEORY OF COMEDY

THE plays of Terence, it is generally accepted, served as a bridge between the old Roman comedy and the modern European comedy of manners. In England, as nowhere else in Europe, a fusion of native art and learned tradition took place, which formed the basis of Shakespearian comedy; but comedy was not destined to play an important part in the literature of Germany where native taste was not robust enough to withstand and blend with the inflow of classical forms, and where there was no intricate network joining the common life with the stage such as existed in Elizabethan and Stuart England.[1] The reasons for this may be various and complex, but they derive from the temperament of the people and from their history.

The Germans have a passion for argument and a tremendous power of concentration, and it was not entirely fortuitous that in their universities scholasticism continued to flourish until late in the seventeenth century. The analytical and deductive method furthered the development of a cast of mind which was strengthened still more by the endless theological discussions during and after the Reformation. The love of argument (sometimes for its own sake) and the ability to concentrate together encouraged persistent probing in a limited field, but at the same time sacrificed variety of interest to rigidity of intellect. The energies of German thinkers and writers were sapped by doctrinal feuds and it was not until the seventeenth century that they displayed interest in the great changes occurring in the different fields of human activity on anything like the scale this had been happening in neighbouring countries. German literature was caught in the vortex of a whirlpool of futile wrangling, whilst abroad European letters reflected the zest in recent discoveries, excitement at the prospect of further progress, and in Elizabethan England intensity of emotion and interest in human nature and the universe. Hence the enormous difference in kind and achievement between English and German literature in the second half of the sixteenth century. Without zest in life there can be no vital literature, certainly no lively comedy. Luther and the Humanists, moreover, had kept a throttle-hold on German writers. The

[1] Cp. M. C. Bradbrook: *The Growth and Structure of Elizabethan Comedy*, p. 17.

Reformer prescribed biblical themes as dramatic material, which were duly and dutifully treated *ad nauseam*.

For the Humanists at the end of the sixteenth century Greek tragedy had a magnetic attraction; the leisurely unfolding of the plot, the meditative manner appealed to the German scholars. It harmonised with their devotion to the search for cause and effect, with the ponderous, painstaking working of their mind. A lively, runaway action was alien to their temperament. Greek tragedy, too, was associated with the theory of Aristotle, and a number of German scholars displayed a distinct partiality for this theoretical approach to literature. Especially did they respond to the organisation and method in Aristotle's *Poetics*. Wimpheling, Vadianus, Rebhun, and Fabricius were a few amongst a host of clergymen and schoolmasters who published tracts on the theory of poetry. In his annotated edition of the *Brothers* (1576) Chytraeus appended his "Propositions" on comedy. The following are of especial interest to us:[1]

> xxxiii. The contents of comedies are the peevishness or indulgence of parents, the goodness or knavery of children, the harmony or discord of married couples, the fidelity or deceits of servants, the diligence or meddlesomeness of citizens, marriages and divorces, prodigality and niggardliness, and very many others of such kind.
>
> xxxix. The end of comedy in general, as likewise with other common forms of poetry, is to imitate aptly and to teach with delight.
>
> xlii. Comedy and tragedy, however, differ from one another, first in the rank of personages, who in comedy are of less account and plebeian, in tragedy noble and royal.
>
> xliii. Second, in the quality of employments and affairs, which in comedy are everyday and often merry, in tragedy truly weighty, difficult, dangerous, and lamentable.
>
> xliv. Third, in the manner of the beginning, which in comedy is usually turbulent, in tragedies quiet.
>
> xlv. Fourth, in the manner of the ending, which in comedy is joyful, in tragedy dreadful.
>
> xlvi. Fifth, in the manner of style, which in comedy is humble and popular, in tragedy serious and removed from vulgar diction.
>
> xlvii. Sixth, comedy is more expressive of character (morata), tragedy more passionate (pathetica).

As it has already been pointed out,[2] the propositions show a characteristic blend of Horace, Donatus, Aristotle, and Melanchthon.

The incursions of the sixteenth-century Humanists into the realm of theory were modest compared with the treatises spawned in the following century. Literally scores were published after Opitz' *Buch von der Deutschen Poeterey* (1624). The comedy as a literary form was, of

---

[1] The translation is that of M. T. Herrick: *Comic Theory in the sixteenth century*, p. 81.

[2] *Ibid.*, p. 80.

course, given short shrift in these compendia. Opitz who followed unswervingly the example of Scaliger and Heinsius decreed that

„Die Comedie . . . redet von . . . betrug und schalckheit der knechte / ruhmrätigen Landtsknechten / buhlersachen / leicht= fertigkeit der jugend / geitze des alters / kuppleren und solchen sachen."[1]

The same opinion was expressed by Elizabethan critics.[2] This view of comedy in Renaissance Europe was different from that of the Middle Ages. When in the thirteenth century Vincent de Beauvais pronounced that

Comedy is a poem changing a sad beginning into a happy ending

he formulated the predominant medieval idea of comedies, which was the converse of the Boethian definition of tragedy.[3] Later, towards the end of the sixteenth and then in the seventeenth century, it was not so much fun for its own sake as ridicule that formed the substance of comedy, with the grand exception of Shakespeare, and in particular of his *Midsummer Night's Dream* where the world is without evil.

The confinement of the action in comedy to the environment of the peasant and servant, which Opitz and others demanded, was accepted in Germany in practice. And not only was there a social barrier between tragedy and comedy, but also formally a rigid separation of the tragic from the comic. When in Gryph's *Peter Squentz* Pickelhäring, having been given the rôle of Piramus, says

Ein Soldat und Buler / so muß ich lachen und sauer sehen.

Peter Squentz warns him:

Aber nicht beydes auff einmahl.

To which Pickelhäring replies

Das ist gut! denn ich kan nicht zugleich lachen und weinen / wie Jehan Potage. Es stehet auch einer so vornehmen Person / wie ich bin / nicht an / sondern ist Närrisch nicht Fürstlich.

What we miss here is the recognition that tragedy and comedy are by no means always divorced in real life. As Walter Benjamin puts it,

---

[1] *Neudrucke*, No. 1, pp. 22 *et seq.*
[2] Cp. Nevill Coghill: The Basis of Shakespearian Comedy in *Essays and Studies*, pp. 7 *et seq.*
[3] Commoedia poesis exordium triste laeto fine commutans. The same conception is implicit in the title of Dante's fourteenth century poem *Divina Commedia* which describes a journey through hell, purgatory, and heaven. Cp. E. K. Chambers: *The Medieval Stage*, p. 209, note.

"Die Komik—richtiger: der reine Spaß—ist die obligate Innenseite
der Trauer, die ab und zu wie das Futter eines Kleides im Saum oder
Revers zur Geltung kommt. Ihr Vertreter ist an den der Trauer
gebunden."[1] Towards the end of the century there are signs of a more
liberal view of the *social* boundaries. In the treatises of Stieler, Masen,
Rotth, and Omeis, for instance, we find concessions in favour of high
personages figuring in comedy, but only if the dignity of the aristocrat is not injured. To this end the language in such *Heldenspiele* could
be elevated "halb prächtig in die Höh'," Rotth, for example, pronounced as follows:

So ist demnach die neue bey uns itzo gebräuchliche Comödie
nichts anders als ein solch Handelungs-Spiel / in welcher entweder
eine lächerliche oder auch wohl löbliche Verrichtung einer Person /
sie sey wer sie wolle / sie sey erdichtet oder aus den Historien
bekant / mit vielen sinnreichen und lustigen Erfindungen auff-
geführet und abgehandelt wird / daß entweder die Zuschauer die
Fehler und Tugenden des gemeinen menschlichen Lebens gleichsam
spielweise erkennen und sich bessern lernen / oder doch sonst zu
einer Tugend auffgemuntert werden.[2]

There was indeed a classical precedent in Plautus' *Amphitruo* to which
the pundits could point in justification of their enlightened attitude.[3]

The primary function of Renaissance comedy was didactic; it was
to edify the audience, but also the actors. This idea was later expressed
cogently by Christian Weise in his essay "Von Verfertigung der
Comödien und ihrem Nutzen" which he wrote as preface to the
Ungleich und gleich gepaarten Liebes-Alliance (1708).[4] We are told that
the comedy affords young people an insight into social and political
life, quickly and easily; that it trains them in deportment, discretion,
wordly wisdom—in short, prepares them for the trials and temptations
that await them in the harsh and sinful world without. The *Schul-
komödie* of which Weise was the outstanding exponent, naturally had
no room for the clown with his crude gestures and rude jokes, which
as Omeis put it, „öffters die Schau-spiele in Sau-spiele verwandeln."[5]

---

[1] *Schriften*, Vol. I, p. 248.
[2] A. C. Rotth: *Vorbereitung zur Deutschen Poesie*, etc., dritter Teil, p. 130.
Interesting light is cast on the interdependence of many of these treatises, if the
above quotation is compared with M. D. Omeis' words on the same subject in
Gründliche Anleitung zur Teutschen accuraten Reim- und Dichtkunst, etc. (1704),
p. 231. The close resemblance of the wording could scarcely be fortuitous.
[3] Cp. Burmeister's adaptation of *Amphitruo* (1621).
[4] The same doctrine appeared in Sir Philip Sidney's *Defense of Poesie*. We
remember, too, that the drama of the schools supplied the later Elizabethan stage
with its literary models, and moulded the habits of actors and audience.
[5] *Op. cit.*, p. 236.

The farcical interludes written to accompany the tragedies, on the other hand, continued to employ the clown. The *Komödie*, a rather comprehensive term in the seventeenth century, was a drama which could not be called a 'tragedy' because it did not bear the seal of violent death. There were in addition a number of alternative designations which tend to be confusing today, since there was virtually no uniformity in their use; but they were all translations of the word *comoedia*, viz. *Freudenspiel, Lustspiel, Scherzspiel, Schimpfspiel*. According to Harsdörffer the *Freudenspiele* were so called „weil ihr Inhalt uñ Ende frölich und lustig ist."[1] They must have a moral, and the characters are types; there may be music, but vocal only if the play is in prose. A *Freudenspiel* was, it seems, sometimes distinguishable from a *Lustspiel* inasmuch as the former was acted by professionals, and the latter by men of rank as amateurs.[2] The *Schimpfspiel* was lower in pitch, blunter in manner, earthier in style and more hilarious in mood. The titlepage of Gryph's *Peter Squentz* read "Absurda Comica oder Herr Peter Squentz / Schimpff=Spiel." The situations and characters are ludicrous; the play is in fact a farce, though perhaps not quite as boisterous as the traditional *Posse*. *Horribilicribrifax* and *Gelibte Dornrose* Gryphius called *Scherzspiele*, and although the social environment here is not the same in each case, both plays are distinctly less noisy and exuberant than *Peter Squentz*.

B. THE OUTLOOK ON LIFE AS A BASIS OF COMEDY

DUALISM is by no means peculiar to the mental experience of seventeenth-century man; the outlook of the medieval European, for example, was dualistic in the sense that there was a gulf between the two forms of existence—earthly and heavenly. By and large, medieval man regarded his allotted span of earthly existence as a period of preparation for the ultimate true life in the company of God. He was constantly aware of the existence of both worlds, but he was not so fascinated by the gulf between them as the man of the Baroque was. This is not to say that he was indifferent to death; the wide appeal of the Morality play proved that it was not so. But for the medieval Christian death was an experience which brought fulfilment —a realisation of the divine promise of eternal life for those deserving it, whereas by the seventeenth century it was symbolised most commonly by the *Sensenmann* bearing the hour glass which measured the

[1] *Poetischer Trichter*, etc. zweiter Teil (1648), p. 94.
[2] Cp. B. Markwardt: *Geschichte der deutschen Poetik*, Vol. I, p. 90.

points in time as they trickled away inevitably and irrevocably.[1] To Gryphius and his contemporaries this Reaper of men did not appear in the first place as the Deliverer who gave a higher permanent life in exchange for a base and transitory existence, but as an unknown, unfathomable, and sinister phenomenon which could and did terminate their physical being at any one moment, once and for all. In the work of Rist and others "Zeitverkürzung" is used for "Todesbetrachtung."[2]

In seventeenth-century Germany the awareness of Time and of the evanescence of earthly life was more intense or at least more frequently and fervently proclaimed than in any previous period. It is a leitmotiv in the lyric and the drama, and at the end of the greatest prose epic of the age Simplicius tells us his life has been „ein ſchwerer Schatten/ . . . ein ſchwerer Traum." The title-page of Ludwig Hollonius' play *Somnium vitae humanae* (1605)[3] warns that the work shows „gleich in einem Spiegel" „das unſer zeitlichs Leben / mit all ſeiner Herrligkeit nur ein nichtiger und betrieglicher Traum ſey." In *Peter Squentz*, from the first discussion of their play to the end of the performance, the transparency of their rôles is repeatedly emphasised. At the beginning of the play Pickelhäring introduces the leitmotiv with the words „es iſt nur zu bejammern / daß es nicht wahr iſt." Kricks urges Klotz-George not to worry about the effectiveness of his make-up, „man weiß doch wol / daß ihr die rechte Thisbe nicht ſeyd." In the prologue to his play Squentz reassures the audience:

Wenn Thisbe ſich ſo wird verletzen /
Sie erſticht ſich nicht / es iſt nur Schimpff (i.e. a prank).

Klipperling announces that he is not a lion at all, but a poor joiner with a crowd of children who has to do his share in this performance for what reward he can get from it. Piramus, about to put an end to his life, sets our mind at rest: „ich erſteche mich nicht recht / es iſt nur Spiel." To the reasons for the louder and more persistent cry of *vanitas*! mentioned above must be added the misery and mass extermination that accompanied the Thirty Years' War. Life then was cruel, precarious, and more liable to sudden reversals of fortune than ever. The theatre, that is dramatic performances in school and market place, became for the many a means of escape from the bleak and discordant realities of day-to-day existence. The comedy presented the foolishness as well as the depravity of men, and for a serious and

[1] Cp. the frontispiece to the 1657 and 1663 editions of Gryph's poetical works, reproduced in my edition of *Carolus Stuardus*.
[2] Cp. J. Rist: *Die alleredelste Zeit-Verkürtzung*, etc. (1668).
[3] Reprinted in *Neudrucke*, No. 95.

-conscientious practitioner like Christian Weise it was „eine Ärßeneŋ des Menſchlichen Elendes."[1]

Both tragedies and comedies had one fundamental feature in common: they postulated and demonstrated the vanity of earthly life. The dedicatory note to Hollonius' play mentioned above is a homily on the text *Vanitas, vanitatum, et omnia vanitas*. The author tells us that he had been casting about for a suitable story as a basis for a drama which should illustrate this text. To his great satisfaction he hit upon a true tale[2] about Philip the Good, Duke of Burgundy (1419–67) who one day came across a helplessly drunken man lying in the gutter. Having ordered his removal to the palace, the duke dressed him in royal clothes, and when he recovered consciousness gave him royal food and drink for a whole day. In the evening the strange guest was pressed so hard to eat and drink that he sank under the table, once more in a drunken stupor. The Duke ordered the man to be clad in his rags again and returned to the gutter where he had been picked up twenty-four hours earlier. Later the bewildered man related his experience to his family as a dream in the night which he knew was not real.

> Dann hie in einem Spiegel flar
> Wird fürgeſtellet offenbar /
> das unſers Lebens Ehr und Macht /
> Frewd / Herligfeit / Ruhm / Zier und pracht
> Seŋ nur ein Traum und falſcher ſchein.

Thus the announcer before the opening of the play. The drama is an allegory based on what the author called a „luſtige Geſchicht" written, however, with deep conviction. For the *vanitas* theme was not just an article of faith, but confirmed, as he says, in „der teglichen Experientz."

In the tragedies the burgher audience saw the deeds and fate of kings and princes—figures remote and far above their own station in life. The comedies, on the other hand, brought them face to face with their own kind or those familiar to them. They saw their own troubles, fears, quarrels, heartaches, as well as their excitement and joy, but as spectators who were aware of the futility of the things of this world. In the comedy of the time the interest generally grows around one or two characters, who, when they overreach themselves and assume a rôle which is not rightly theirs, appear ludicrous. This kind of comedy stems partly from the social consciousness of the period. As we have

---

[1] *Tobias und die Schwalbe*, IV, 4. *Zittauisches Theatrum* (1683), p. 347.

[2] A version of the story appears in the *Arabian Nights* (Harun Alrashid was the prince and Abu Hassan the beggar), and was later to be the theme of Weise's *Niederländische Bauer* (1685). Cp. a similar motif in *The Taming of the Shrew* and in Hauptmann's *Schluck und Jau*.

seen, the structure of society was believed to be divinely ordained; hence it was folly to attempt to upset it.

Der Bauer wohnet recht / wo er die Ochsen treibt.
Dem Bauer wird kein Dienst mit unsrer Pracht gethan /

Such is the pronouncement of the courtiers at the end of Weise's *Niederländische Bauer*.[1] „Lebt ihr fein erbar nur / und bleibt in euren Stande" says Fidel to Frau Schlampampe's daughters after their abortive attempts to pose as ladies of rank in Reuter's play.[1] The most successful of the comedies of Heinrich Julius is about Vincentius Ladislaus, an eccentric ex-soldier and incorrigible braggart, who by his pretentiousness and falsehoods leads a life which is one colossal illusion. He is in reality a poor, ignorant, timid individual but he feigns to be of noble stock, learned, accomplished, courageous, and a bold adventurer. At the end of the play this prince of impostors is unmasked and laughed to scorn by people who know their station in life and keep to it. At the end of Gryph's *Horribilicribrifax* the two swaggering officers are soundly trounced by a mere servant, and exposed as miserable poltroons.[2] Reuter's Schelmuffsky is another well-known instance of the charlatan. The braggart soldier was of course a type already familiar in the works of Plautus, but the popularity of this character in seventeenth-century German comedy does not signify wholesale borrowing from the Roman poet. Horribilicribrifax and Daradiridatumtarides with their affected mannerisms, extravagant clothes, their smattering of foreign languages, had a special significance in an age when there was a very strong conviction abroad that earthly life was as unreal and impermanent as the rôle of the actor—and of the impostor.

C. LAUGHING MATTER IN COMEDY

LAUGHTER, as we have already said, comes from the contrast between truth and pretence, ideality and reality, and as this had a greater fascination in the seventeenth century than in any previous period in recorded history, it is not surprising that this proved to be the age of great European comedy. In Germany comedy now had a metaphysical basis which was lacking in the Shrovetide plays and farces of Hans Sachs and his contemporaries. Obscenities and horseplay became less frequent; instead interest in human personality and in

[1] Reprinted in Die deutsche Barockkomödie, *Reihe Barock*.

[2] It is, I think, wrong to speak of Gryph's acceptance of the social order as 'snobbery', as does H. Wichert (*J. B. Schupp and the Baroque Satire in Germany*, p. 43 *et passim*).

man's place in the universe grew. In Germany both tragedy and comedy are at last beginning to be informed with the excitement that spread abroad in an epoch of numerous and great discoveries.[1] This participation in recent and sensational additions to knowledge nourished the mendacity of the mountebank; but the sudden overthrow of ancient theories concerning the universe, e.g. the ptolemaic, also sharpened the interest in the problem of what was true, and what illusory. In many of the comedies the genuine and the counterfeit appear side by side. Gryph's Dornrose is contrasted with Salome; Horribilicribrifax and Daradiridatumtarides and Sempronius with Cleander and Palladius; Selene with Sophia. The Vincentius Ladislaus of Heinrich Julius shows off before the Duke Silvester who actually possesses the qualities of which the 'hero' boasts in vain.

The folly of men and women, their weakness for posing and imposing, for deceit and pretence, is laid bare in these plays. But by and large the poet does not treat his wayward children harshly. He laughs at them, we laugh at them (though perhaps not always for the same reason). Sometimes we may imagine the author is angry, but his temper is always under control; he remonstrates by means of ridicule, not fierce denunciation. His treatment is burlesque, sometimes derisive, but rarely vicious;[2] his comedy not intellectual, but comedy of manners and of situation. In the Prologue to his *Bäurischer Machiavellus* Weise states bluntly: „Es ist ein schlechtes Thun / wenn ein vergift'ter Hohn den Nächsten schänden soll." After watching the antics of Peter Squentz and his crew, Theodorus leaves with the words: „Wir sind müder vom Lachen als vom Zusehen." *Horribilicribrifax* and *Gelibte Dornrose* finish with a dance. The end of these plays seems to confirm that they were written in a mood of fun. But the characters whose personality and behaviour move us to laughter take themselves very seriously; that is, of course, one primary cause of our mirth—the gulf between what they try to be, and what they in fact are—something of which on occasions they seem completely unaware. The persons at whom Gryphius pokes fun are pompous and full of their own importance. They have their counterpart in the martyr heroes of the contemporary tragedy, who are unshakably convinced of their righteousness. The stubbornness with which the comic characters persist in their behaviour, like the steadfastness of the martyrs in the *Kunstdrama*, is a form of the self-assertion so characteristic of the Baroque personality. Such may not have been Gryph's own view, and he probably did not see the affinity

---

[1] In England three times as many comedies as tragedies were performed on the Elizabethan stage.

[2] It is in his sonnets and epigrams that Gryphius castigates men of his own social class for their deceit, dishonesty, and so on.

between the pretentious dignity he made fun of, and the imperious pose in the sculpture and painting of the time which was taken seriously. What he did was to reproduce from his environment, with a certain licence, people and situations which amused him. For this reason the plays of Gryphius and of Rist, Reuter, and Weise are valuable sources for a study of seventeenth-century German society. Weise, again in the Prologue to his *Bäurischer Machiavellus*, tells the audience:

Nur diefes magft du ftets von mir verfichert fein /
Daß ich dich immerfort zur Luft vexieren werde;
Du bift des Lachens Zweck.

Perhaps the most striking feature of human behaviour in seventeenth century Germany was extravagance. It was an age of dangerous and brilliant living. Life was cheap, the national economy topsy-turvy, and perhaps never before had there been side by side such extremities of cowering wretchedness and brazen splendour. If the long and disastrous war had done much to affect the tone of life, it was by no means entirely responsible for it. Society in Germany, as elsewhere in Europe, was very rank-conscious. As we saw above, each class and profession was extremely jealous of its status and privileges, and proud of any advancement. This latter was a goal which many individuals would reach (or appear to reach) at any price, including their integrity; and as this was an epoch where exaggeration was the keynote of every form of human activity—dress, deportment, speech, art, and literature—the conduct of charlatans and parvenus was ostentatious to the point of being grotesque. Consequently if German Baroque comedy were purged of its braggarts, it would be emasculated. Without their garish clothes and jewellery (most of it counterfeit) it would be drab and lifeless. As for the peasants, as a whole they had no social ambition. Where they appear in the drama, it is their ugliness, their crude demeanour and speech and coarse humour which provide the comic element.[1] Amongst the socially conscious, on the other hand, titles were at a premium. A more uncompromising exposure of this foible than the opening lines of *Peter Squentz* it would be difficult to find in contemporary literature. No withering sarcasm here; in fact one has the feeling that now and then Gryphius suffers his fools gladly. The authors of German comedy could and did castigate the vices of men,

---

[1] Cp. mod. German *Tölpel*. In England, too, people laughed at 'deformed creatures' who today would fill us with dismay if not revulsion. Cp. Thomas Wilson's *Art of Rhetoric* (1553), and Sidney's *Defense of Poesie* (circa 1580). W. Benjamin comments: "Selten, vielleicht auch nie gab sich die spekulative Ästhetik Rechenschaft davon, wie nah der strenge Spaß dem Grauenhaften liegt. Wer sah nicht Kinder lachen, wo Erwachsene sich entsetzen?" (*ibid.*).

but in spite of Weise's indebtedness to Molière, ignorance and foolish eccentricities were apt to be presented so as to produce a hearty laugh, rather than subjected to the polished but mordant wit dominant in French classical comedy.

For a variety of reasons—geographical, historical, political, and social—seventeenth-century Germany was very susceptible to foreign influences. In this respect again the War was a contributory factor. French and Spanish soldiery left their mark on the German language as well as on other aspects of the native way of life. It became fashionable, for instance, to interlard one's speech with foreign words and phrases as evidence of culture and *bon ton*. Thus Horribilicribrifax and his comrade-in-arms scarcely complete a sentence without Italian or French words. (Altogether seven languages are represented in this play.) In Reuter's *Ehrliche Frau* a number of the characters have this mannerism; the lowlier their station the more ridiculous these foreign words sounded. When both misused and misunderstood, they were doubly laughable.

THE COMEDIES OF ANDREAS GRYPHIUS

IN his preface to *Sterbender Cato* (1732) Gottsched wrote: "Ich fragte
ihn (den Prinzipal der Dresdner Hofkomödianten) sonderlich warum
man nicht Andr. Gryphii Trauerspiele . . . aufführe. Die Antwort
fiel, daß er die erstern auch sonst vorgestellet hätte: Allein itzo ließe
sichs nicht mehr thun. Man würde solche Stücke in Versen nicht mehr
sehen wollen: Zumal sie gar zu ernsthaft wären und keine lustige
Person in sich hätten." As inaugurator of the *Kunsttragödie* with its
severely classical form Gryphius excluded the comic element from
serious drama. In this respect he was in accord with Opitz who insisted
that tragedy and comedy be kept separate. The attitude of both men
was consistent with the social order of their time, and the drama advocated by the one and written by the other reflected this order. Comedy
concerned the doings of commoners and was not allowed to intrude
into works about the fate of those in high places. The converse, however, did not hold; royalty and the nobility do appear, but only in the
background of, say, *Peter Squentz* and *Horribilicribrifax*. They are the
norm against which the behaviour of the characters is seen in relief.[1]
This situation again had its counterpart in real life; the prince's residence was closed to the populace, but the sovereign could at will move
among his humbler subjects.

It should be remembered that in the seventeenth century men were
able to live in what Sir Thomas Browne called "divided and distinguished worlds."[2] This meant that their work often had an amphibious
nature. Gryphius for example delighted in scientific experiment con-
ducted on modern lines, and at the same time lectured on chiromancy,
and practised astrology; he wrote devotional poetry and prurient
verse. Thus it is not surprising that he turned his hand both to high
tragedy and low comedy. His comedies, of course, had no pretensions
to be works of art, but I think he enjoyed writing them. They have not
the discipline of form that distinguishes the tragedies, and he may well
have been nervous about the effect they would have on his reputation
as a poet.[3] At all events they show him to have had keen powers of

[1] I cannot, then, agree with Gundolf when he writes: "Der zuschauende
Herzog und seine Hofleute bedeuten nichts, da sie fast stumme Personen sind."
(*Shakespeare und der deutsche Geist*, p. 79.)

[2] An account of Gryph's life, personality, and outlook on life is to be found in
the Introduction to my edition of *Carolus Stuardus*.

[3] A considerable number of years elapsed between the writing of *Squentz* and
Horribilicribrifax and their publication. Cp. pp. lv *et seq.*

observation and an affection for the humbler folk around him with all their foibles and limitations. The atmosphere in the tragedies is rarified; the heroes are ethereal, at least when we first see them they have inwardly taken leave of this world. The comedies, written probably when the author was in exuberant spirits, are earthy and present the natural impulses, crude instincts, shallow pretence, and insatiable ambition Gryphius encountered whichever way he turned. The figures in these comedies remind us for the most part of kinds of people which still exist to-day, though in different guise. In many cases they are very close to being embodiments of vanity, arrogance, ignorance, incontinence, modesty, wisdom, chastity, and so on. They are characterised with bold strokes—and occasionally a delicate nuance—and it is their vitality, not the plot, that makes the play. The discharged officer turned up everywhere in Germany at the end of the Thirty Years' War, and was ever ready to boast of his fabulous deeds and experiences. In Gryph's hands he is exaggerated and made to look ridiculous; of the peasants in *Dornrose* we can say at least that they lose nothing of their actual clumsy strength and uncouthness, nor do the mechanicals in *Squentz*; whilst Cyrilla is as macabre an old hag as we should wish to see. The plot in the comedies is loose, and sometimes (*Horribilicribrifax* and *Dornrose*) disjointed. Scene is apt to follow scene apparently at random, and we are interested not so much in where events are leading us, as in what the characters will have to say next, and how they will bear themselves in different situations.[1]

The ramshackle structure of Gryph's comedies was common to those German plays which were not entirely in the learned tradition. The reason for this was the failure of authors to become good playwrights, that is artificers who could adapt to dramatic form the narrative material on which they drew. Since the Middle Ages the principal literary tradition had been narrative—even in the old Morality and Mystery plays. What secular drama existed was cultivated in the schools and in the scholarly classical tradition, i.e. it was well-ordered and formal.[2] If the two traditions had been successfully amalgamated, there would have been the basis for a national tragedy and comedy. But the great achievement of the Elizabethans had no counterpart in Germany. Indeed the distinctive qualities of German plays were not concentration, intensity, cohesion, but diffuseness, profuseness, discursiveness. In other words, not only did the narrative habit prove too strong for German dramatists, but they were unaware of the opportunity deriving from a fusion of the two traditions—the secular-dramatic and

---

[1] In our own day this largely unmotivated succession of scenes brings to mind the technique in Brecht's 'epic theatre'.

[2] Cp. Madeleine Doran: *Endeavors of Art*, Chap. 10.

religious-narrative. Their primary concern was moral content and didactic function. The title-page of Andreas Hartmann's *Lutherus redivivus* (1624) offers a broad hint of the chaotic structure of such plays: "This is a true description (*sic*) of the birth, arrival, life, profession, office, and teaching . . . of Martin Luther . . . done into a very fine, charming, and Christian comedy." The hymn-writer Martin Rinckhart wrote a 'drama' which, so the title-page tells us, depicts the Peasant War "not only as a drama, but also as a real and entertaining historical compendium."[1]

If the structure of Gryph's comedies is haphazard, the character delineation, as we have already suggested, is forthright and vigorous, for such qualities as the crude and extravagant in speech and behaviour, when exaggerated, made the poet and his audience laugh. The latter, we remember, was drawn from the educated section of the middle class in touch with the schools where Gryph's plays were performed. They could understand and appreciate the half-dozen or so foreign languages introduced into *Horribilicribrifax*, and the gross blunders which Peter Squentz made when showing off his 'scholarship.' Yet Gryph's comedy was not of the intellectual kind which provokes a smile of delicate amusement.

It is important to recall at this point that our response today to a reading or performance of these plays is not always exactly that of Gryph's audience. They had different values and ideals, and their outlook was by no means the same as that of a twentieth-century audience. Gryphius represented the burgher element in society which set great store by elegance of speech, grace in deportment and manners, and a solid fund of classical learning—a class which was very conscious of its status and of the gulf which separated it from the lower orders. I suggest that an audience representative of such standards, when confronted with the abusive language and obscene invective of social outcasts, the lumbering animalism of the peasant, the transparent pretence to learning of the village 'scholar,' laughed, not sardonically but with genuine and light-hearted amusement, because they knew themselves to be secure against such folly. When the depraved village schoolmaster threatens Cyrilla the old hag,

    Jch wil dir den Ars an deine Zunge wischen

and she counters with

    Jch wil dein Maul unter ein Scheißhaus nageln

This struck the cultured spectators of the time not as simply obscene, as an audience of today would doubtless consider it, but (just like

[1] *Monetarius Seditiosus* (1625).

Cyrilla's reading of obscenities into Sempronius' Latin tags)[1] as up-roariously funny, coming from such flotsam and jetsam of society. The norm against which such behaviour was judged remained the mode of life of a devout, scholarly, and respectable citizen. The use of dialect was perfectly natural to the peasantry; few could speak any other form of German, and an educated person hearing them registered no sur-prise. When, however, this dialect was spoken on stage before an audience of cultured burghers and aristocrats, they were at once conscious of themselves and their standards, and the contrast was a source of merriment.

Majuma and Piastus, although published as Freudenspiel and Lust- und Gesangspiel respectively, were really composed as festive plays for royal occasions. The former has an idyllic, mythological setting, borrowed from Ovid, and is written in rhymed couplets of varying rhythm. Only the crippled soldier has the least affinity with any of the charac-ters of what we might call the genuine comedies. In Piastus one of the dukes appears in person in the company of angels, priests, and princes. This guarantees the dignity of the play. Even the short scene introdu-cing the Knechte and Mägde has no hint of impropriety. Their be-haviour is jubilant, but not abandoned. The Verlibte Gespenste was also written for a special occasion—the marriage of the Duke of Lignitz and Brieg to a high-born lady whom Gryphius had known personally for some time. The play is about the power of love, and Gryphius wished to demonstrate it on two levels, the burgher and the peasant. By means of the Mischspiel, in which an act of each play alternated with the other, he was able to do this and at the same time keep the more representative of the two socially intact.

Gryph's comedy, I think, derives more from his naturalistic treat-ment, or rather from his drastic exposure of human folly than from an irrepressible sense of the comic. Its success rests on his mastery of language. He was probably not a wag; his comedy is on the whole sensuous, not comedy of the intellect. It does not proceed from a sus-tained pattern of thought, but directly from what we see and hear in successive doses, although the vanitas idea is always in the background. He presented people as he saw them, allowing himself here and there a

---

[1] Zuckmayer's Seelenbräu offers an instance in contemporary literature of comedy deriving from a similar misunders anding of foreign words: "Weshalb?" schrie der Professor empört. "Weil's eine Schand is! Da könnt' a jeder kommen und sagen, es ist Musik, wenn er auf'n Soachdeckel (= Seichdeckel, Klosett-deckel) haut!" . . . Es handle sich um eine unverschämte, frivole und stümper-hafte Kakophonie. "So a Gemeinheit," sagte der Ammetsberger, der glaubte, daß eine "Kakophonie" etwas Obszönes sein müsse. (Cp. kacken = to go to stool.) Obscenities are, of course, not unknown in twentieth-century drama. One may recall, for example, Brecht's early plays.

little licence, especially with fantastic personalities like Horribilicribri-fax, but making no *essential* modifications. Each character speaks according to his station in life, and the nuances in character delineation are sometimes quite subtle, but the contrast between what is and what should be, between reality and ideality is indispensable to these plays. In the *Mischspiel* Gryphius adopted the device of intermingling a drama in dialect prose with one in elegant verse, and used it with marked comic effect. Dornrose alone amongst the peasantry speaks High German; her personality is thereby enhanced and she forms a link between the two plays.

In the comedies, then, the poet's treatment differs from that in the tragedies where the characters are either 'good' or 'bad' or wholly without personality. Whereas the tragedies are idealistic, the plays we have just been discussing present real, contemporary life. Here, too, the poet assumes a certain moral responsibility; little or no moralising in the comedies themselves, but the outcome is what Gryphius himself considered to be just. Here is an important reason why, to a twentieth-century audience, these plays may seem deficient in comedy. Nowa-days the author is not expected to sit in judgment on the personalities in his comedies. Indeed such an attitude would be considered irrelevant and disturbing.

PETER SQUENTZ

A. SOURCE

THERE has been a variety of opinion on the sources to which Gryphius was indebted for his *Peter Squentz*. Gottsched wrote: "Ob wohl der Verfasser in diesem Stücke nicht so ehrlich, als in der Vorrede des vorigen (i.e. *Säugamme*) gestanden, woher er es entlehnt hat: so ist es dennoch eine ausländische Erfindung. In Shakespeares Summer Nights-Day (*sic*) ist ein Zwischenspiel eingeschaltet, das den Schulmeister Quince nennet. Das ist unser Squenz, doch hat Gryph viel hinzugesetzet, und alles auf deutschen Fuß eingerichtet."[1] J. E. Schlegel[2] insisted more precisely on Gryph's indebtedness to Shakespeare. Now it is extremely doubtful whether Gryphius ever knew Shakespeare's plays directly, and indeed one looks in vain in his work for a mention of the English poet's name.[3] It seems that Gottsched did Gryphius an injustice by accusing him of concealing his source, for in his preface to *Peter Squentz* Gryphius writes of the number of performances of *Squentz* plays which had already taken place in Germany, and of the persons who had no scruples about claiming to be the inventor of the *Squentz* material. He goes on to give to the Altdorf professor Daniel Schwenter the credit for the first performance in Germany of a *Squentz* play. Far from concealing his debt to another writer, Gryphius tells us explicitly that it was Schwenter's play on which he based his own.[4] As to the source of Schwenter's version, the controversy over the last hundred and fifty years has been inconclusive.[5]

[1] *Nöthiger Vorrath zur Geschichte der Deutschen Dramatischen Dichtkunst*, etc. (1757), p. 217.
[2] *Werke*, dritter Teil (1764), p. 31.
[3] As late as 1682 D. G. Morhof, one of the literary pundits, confessed that he had read nothing by Shakespeare. Cp. *Unterricht von der teutschen Sprache und Poesie*.
[4] *Saradin und Violandra*, a play attributed to Schwenter, may have been the title of his *Squentz* play. Violandra is the name of the princess in Gryph's play, and "Serenus" bears some resemblance to "Saradin".
[5] Early in the nineteenth century Bredow denied that it was Shakespeare's play, and claimed that the substance of *Peter Squentz* was "ächt altdeutsch." (G. G. Bredow: *Nachgelassene Schriften*, p. 104.) C. H. Schmid (*Nekrolog der vornehmsten deutschen Dichter*, Vol. I (1785), p. 122) believed it to have a French origin. Tieck thought that Schwenter's source might have been R. Cox's *Bottom the Weaver*, and that Cox himself was indebted to Shakespeare (*Deutsches Theater*, preface to Vol. II). Albert Cohn (*Shakespeare in Germany*, pp. cxxxi–cxxxiii) believed that Gryph's play stemmed directly from Shakespeare. Kollewijn (*Über die Quelle des*

At all events it seems most likely that the *Squentz* material was brought over to Germany by English strolling players.[1] In the decade or so immediately after Shakespeare's death the mention of comedies entitled *Piramus and Thisbe* and *The Merry Conceits of Bottom the Weaver* suggests that the Yokels' play had won a separate existence in England.[2] Perhaps there were two major reasons for this: firstly, the popularity of these clowns and their 'tragedy'; and secondly, the rise of the 'drolls' or 'humours.' The closing of the English theatres in 1642 brought an increase in the number of drolls which were for the most part a patchwork of scenes from recent plays, performed on improvised stages in fairgrounds and inns. One Robert Cox seems to have been associated with such productions.[3] It is quite possible that on his way

---

Peter Squentz—Schnorrs Archiv für Litt. Gesch., Vol. IX, pp. 445 *et seq.*) suggested that Gryph's *Peter Squentz* and the Dutch poet Gramsbergen's *Hartoog van Pierlepon* were based on the same garbled version of the scenes in *A Midsummer Night's Dream*. F. Burg (*Über die Entwicklung des Peter Squentz-Stoffes bis Gryphius—Ztschr. f.d. Altertum & d. Lit.*, Vol. XXV, pp. 130–170) doubted that Gramsbergen's and Gryph's had the same origin.

[1] M. Fürstenau, *op. cit.*, erster Teil, p. 205 mentions several performances by English players of the "Possenspiel von Pyramus und Thisbe" in Dresden in 1660.

[2] The story of Piramus and Thisbe, quite apart from the *Squentz* theme, was of course internationally known thanks to Ovid's *Metamorphoses* and to the *Gesta Romanorum*. In Germany it provided the theme for at least three dramas (in *Knittelverse*) between 1581 and 1607 (ed. A. Schaer: *Drei deutsche Pyramus-Thisbe-Spiele*). The title-page of the MS of *Pyramus und Thisbe* composed in 1581 by an unknown writer mentions Ovid as the author of the story. Likewise Damian Türckis in his play on the same theme, circa 1607. The Straßburg pastor Samuel Israel declares Ovid to be the source of his play, circa 1601. According to K. Trautmann (*Archiv für Lit. Gesch.*, Vol. XI, p. 626), at the beginning of the seventeenth century (e.g. 1604 in Nördlingen) an English version of the play was being performed in the country. This may have derived from Shakespeare's *Dream*, but as we know the anonymous MS mentioned above was completed fifteen to twenty years before the *Dream*, to regard the English play as the source, direct or indirect, of the other two German versions would seem, in the absence of other evidence, unjustified. Rist in his *Aller Edelste Belustigung* (1666), pp. 88–115, tells of the performance of *Piramus and Thisbe* by a troupe of English Comedians which he witnessed in his youth, probably in Bremen or Hamburg. The English players wished to satirise their rivals—a group of local craftsmen led by a "Phantast, der ehemahlen ein Dorffschulmeister gewesen." Consequently in the English Comedians' play a group of rough artisans perform the sketch on the occasion of a royal wedding. The fable had indeed become a part of German folklore long since. Several of the old *Tageweisen* and *Wächterlieder* were about the "Abendgang," the "Grafen beim Brunnen," the "Königstochter und dem jungen Grafen," and so on. Schaer (*op. cit.*, pp. xiv *et seq.*) has uncovered interesting similarities between some of these old songs and the plays he edited. This was possibly what Bredow had in mind when he used the epithet "ächt altdeutsch" (cp. above).

[3] In Restoration England *A Midsummer Night's Dream*, when performed as a

home from the grand tour Gryphius witnessed in Holland a performance of Gramsbergen's play which we know had been produced in
Amsterdam by 1650.[1] It certainly appears that the name "Bulla
Butäin" in the German play and "Bollebebijn" in the Dutch version
are both a corruption of Shakespeare's "Bully Bottom,"[2] either through
the spoken word, or because of the misreading of a manuscript. When
Piramus stabs himself with the hilt of his sword, goes on talking after
he has breathed his last, and at the end carries Thisbe off stage; when
Thisbe stabs herself under her clothes—these are touches reminiscent of
the English strolling players who were ever ready to sacrifice serious
effect for the sake of the comic and of the applause of the audience.
In the "Zuschrift" to his *belobte und beliebte Krieg* written about the
middle of the century, Balthasar Schupp mentioned the performance of
a *Piramus and Thisbe* play by craftsmen in Nürnberg. It is quite possible
that this piece was the self-same play by Schwenter who, until his death
in 1636, was a professor in Altdorf some twenty miles from Nürnberg.
Whatever the progress of the Quince scenes on the continent before
they attracted Gryph's attention, the correspondence in details between
Shakespeare's work and Gryph's is as close as to render it certain that
the English play was the *ultimate* source of *Peter Squentz*.[3]

B. PLOT

THE play opens with all the mechanicals on stage. Peter Squentz,
schoolmaster and scribe, appears as the leader of this group of
craftsmen, and as he calls their names, prefixing each with a
resounding and pretentious title, they answer laconically in monosyl-
lables: „der bin ich." Not only is the contrast laughable, but we notice
with amusement that not one of them expresses surprise at hearing his
title. When the roll has been called, Squentz, with a magnificently
elaborate piece of preciosity, bids them sit down and pay attention. To
his own name he attaches (as yet) no titles, but, so he reminds us, he
possesses plenty of them. It is Pickelhäring (the first of the mechanicals

whole, was coldly received except when it was produced as opera and spectacle,
and in the following century the audience rejected the play in which fairies,
clowns, and aristocrats rubbed shoulders. The drama as an entirety would
certainly not have established itself in seventeenth-century Germany, if it had
ever been imported at that time.

[1] Cp. Kollewijn, *op. cit.*, p. 445.
[2] Cp. the beginning of Act III of *A Midsummer Night's Dream*.
[3] The most striking evidence emerges from a comparison of the first scene of
our play with Act I, Sc. 2 and Act III, Sc. 1 of *A Midsummer Night's Dream*.

to be named) who introduces Squentz with a few witty sentences, the last of which thrusts deeply to the core of Gryph's dramas:

„es ift nur 3u bejammern / daß es nicht wahr ift."

The world is a stage on which the colossal illusion is played. . . . Now it has come to Squentz's ears that their king is fond of the theatre; consequently as the local schoolmaster he is planning to produce a play in the presence of the sovereign himself. This would be an opportunity, he thinks, to stage a memorable performance which would be a credit to them all—and in particular to the producer himself. The suggestion is received enthusiastically. Klotz-George thinks Squentz's choice of play *Piramus und Thisbe* is excellent; it has a good moral and would be sure both to console and admonish the audience. Immediately after this pronouncement Klotz-George admits he does not yet know the plot! Squentz is only too glad to display his learning, but no sooner has he commenced to describe the source of the story, than we recognise in him a charlatan. Ovid, the poet who was frowned upon by the Church, he calls „der Heilige alte Kirchen=Lehrer." The *Metamorphoses*, in the fourth book of which the story of Piramus and Thisbe appears, is corrupted to "Memoriumphosis." When Squentz has given his men the gist of the plot, they discuss the distribution of parts, just as in Shakespeare's play. Klotz-George declares that whoever plays the lion should announce at the outset, for the sake of pregnant women among the spectators, that he is not really a lion, but only, say, Meister Klotz the joiner. When they have decided on a substitute for the lion's skin, they go on to the next problem: will the moon shine on the night of the performance, as it did in Ovid's account, and how can they procure an artificial moon? Eventually they resolve to use a lantern attached to a pike, which could be lowered or extinguished, when the moon hides her face at Thisbe's death. The wall presents the next obstacle. This is important because it is through the chink in the wall that the lovers Piramus and Thisbe converse. Bullabutäin volunteers to play this part by fixing paper to a frame, carrying it on stage and announcing himself as the wall. The most exalted rôle in the comedy is allotted to Pickelhäring—an interesting piece of evidence of the status enjoyed by this figure in the contemporary theatre. As Piramus he must be nobleman, soldier, and lover, that is gay and morose, but not on any account both at the same time; for he is Pickelhäring not Jean Potage, and cannot laugh and weep at once. Moreover it would not become him in the rôle of Piramus, a person of rank. Klotz-George is given the part of Thisbe and is urged not to worry about camouflaging his beard, „man weiß doch wol / daß ihr die rechte Thisbe nicht feyd." Lollinger is called upon to be the fountain at which the lovers are to meet. Gryph's specific mention of the fountain on Ninus's tomb as rendezvous, rather than the tomb itself, provided the motive for the immodesty traditional in the farce. Now that each has his part, the only remaining question is the classification of the play in the announcement. Shall they call it a tragedy or comedy? They decide to compromise and call it „ein ſchön Spiel luſtig und traurig." Meanwhile the text of the play has to be completed, and Squentz enlists the aid of Lollinger the Meistersinger to advise him on the rhyme and metre. The first act closes with a piece of comic miming.

At the beginning of the second act King Theodorus, after a busy session at the Imperial Diet asks his marshal what entertainment he has arranged for the evening. The marshal replies that he has engaged Squentz and his company to perform a play. The performance, he says, promises well, as he has witnessed a rehearsal. Squentz gives them the choice from twelve plays, the last of which bears his own name as author.[1] Squentz is summoned to the royal presence, and when questioned about his origin and status, delivers himself of a piece of verbal nonsense reminiscent of, but by no means as brilliant as the fooling of Shakespeare's court jesters. He is then asked about his repertory and it transpires that of the twelve plays they have offered, they can play only one, viz. *Piramus und Thisbe*. This, Squentz emphasises, is all his own work, as yet neither printed nor performed, in fact just completed. Squentz strongly recommends his own play, much to the amusement of the king and his court.

The third act, which constitutes the bulk of the play, brings the performance of *Piramus und Thisbe*. Squentz introduces it with the verbal buffoonery traditional in the rôle of the announcer or speaker of the prologue to popular plays. He outlines the plot in *Knittelversen*, which remind the queen of the doggerel of the old *Pritschmeister*. His play, he says, has five acts, of which he composed three and Meister Lollinger two—a preposterous claim since the performance turns out to be hopelessly chaotic without any suggestion of 'acts,' and with the loose narrative form characteristic of the old popular plays. The play begins with the entry of Wall who is followed by Piramus. The origin of Wall was the partition separating Piramus' room from his lover's. Piramus accuses Wall of keeping him from Thisbe, and attacks him in a fit of rage. After a short scuffle, Wall is rescued by Squentz, but only after his paper and frame have been battered and torn. Thisbe now appears sighing with love for Piramus, and wishing Wall were not there to separate them. She suddenly notices there is a hole in the partition, and peeping through she espies Piramus. They find they can talk to each other and arrange to meet by moonlight that evening.

[1] Cp. Commentary.

After a lingering farewell—each taking several peeps at the other—they depart, followed by Wall. Now Moon appears (Meister Kricks with a lantern on a pole) and explains that later on Thisbe kills herself by his light. Fountain comes on next singing his song. He is followed by Lion who immediately assures his audience that he is not really a wild beast but merely Klipperling the joiner. Thisbe now arrives at her rendezvous to await Piramus. When she catches sight of Lion, she flees in terror leaving her cloak behind. An argument now develops between Lion and Moon; they come to blows, upset Fountain, and when Squentz intervenes to restore order, he too is thoroughly trounced. The rumpus eventually subsides, that is after a delay brought about by the disappearance of Piramus who has departed in search of a drink! When Piramus returns, he notices Thisbe's cloak near Fountain, believes he sees blood on it and imagines his lady has been mauled to death by Lion. He toys with the idea of suicide, wishes he had not left his sword behind, and when he discovers he has it after all, assures the audience that he will only *pretend* to kill himself. After considerable hesitation he makes as though to stab himself—but with the hilt of the sword—and "dies". At this Moon's light goes out, and Thisbe appears once more in search of her lover. She stumbles over his body, and thinking him asleep, kisses him, whereupon the "dead" Piramus himself tries to steal a kiss. Gradually it dawns on her that her lover is dead, and she implores him to speak to her once more. The "dead" Piramus replies that he cannot oblige because he has no more words in his part. Squentz the producer intervenes to admonish Piramus for speaking when he is no longer alive. Piramus, however, speaks up again, this time agreeing to be silent. Thisbe, thoroughly disconsolate, decides on suicide, "stabs" herself (under her dress) with Piramus' sword, and collapses on his body. Moon and Fountain go off in silence. Piramus gets up, Thisbe leaps on to his shoulders and both depart. Squentz speaks the Epilogue which is as farcical in tone and content as the play itself. Squentz now approaches the king for what he calls the „Xrand̄= gelᴅ." The king asks him how many blunders they have made in their performance, and ultimately decides to pay them fifteen gulden for each blunder. As Squentz observes, it is for their mistakes that they are rewarded, not for their art and skill.

C. THE SUBSTANCE OF THE PLAY

Eubulus: . . und zweiffele nicht / ihre Majeſtät werden ſich
ob der guten Leute Einfalt und wunderlichen Erfindungen
nicht wenig erluſtigen.   (Act II)

Serenus: Hilff Gott das find treffliche Vers.
Caſſandra: Nach Art der alten Pritſchmeiſter Reymen.
Theodorus: Wenn ſie beſſer wären / würden wir ſo ſehr nicht
drüber lachen. (Act III)

"PETER SQUENTZ" is a rollicking farce which can be enjoyed
simply for the tomfoolery of Squentz and his crew. The literary
historian, however, finds that it sheds light on the sense of the
comic which animated an educated audience in seventeenth-century
Germany, and that it consequently merits a place in the history of
German comedy. At the very beginning of the play when the mood is
already mischievous, Lollinger is introduced as „Leinweber und Meiſter=
Sänger." We may remember that the man who first instructed Hans
Sachs in the intricacies of the Meistergesang was Leonhard Nonnenbeck,
a linen weaver whose name seems to be echoed by Lollinger.[1] (The
weavers, together with the shoemakers and furriers, appear to have
been the most enthusiastic practitioners of the Meistergesang.) Sachs
himself is mentioned in the second act, and when writing his play
Squentz calls in Lollinger to help him with the technique of versifica-
tion—a reference to the Tabulatur, i.e. the set of rules and penalties for
their infringement which governed the composition of the Meistergesang. . . . Squentz introduces the play with a prologue. His very
first lines, spoken from memory or extempore are abominable, but
when he finds the paper with his words, we notice that the verse is
much more regular. It reminds the queen of the doggerel of the old
Pritschmeister.

In his Buch von der Deutschen Poeterey Opitz had declared war on the
Knittelvers. According to him „iſt auch ein jeder verß entweder ein
iambicus oder trochaicus . . . das wir aus den accenten unnd dem
thone erkennen / welche ſylbe hoch unnd welche niedrig geſetzt ſoll
werden."[2] As his little book was written generally to formalise
German literature, he insists on regularity in the metre. In his preface
Opitz tells us he wrote the work at the request of various people,
including "vornehme Leute," and implies that his views were held at
the time, if not widely, then by persons with authority in Germany.
He was probably right in this despite the coolness of a Werder, Weck-
herlin, and Schupp, for there was a general trend amongst the new
'aristocracy' of writers in Germany towards a more refined and dis-
ciplined literature such as the grammarians in France, Holland, and

---

[1] F. M. v. Waldeck, op. cit., has, I find, also made this suggestion: Lollinger
was probably one of the characters which, as Gryphius tells us in his preface, he
added to Schwenter's version.

[2] Op. cit., p. 40.

elsewhere had advocated for generations. Indeed, the popular *Knittel-verse* with their indefinite number of unaccented syllables were by no means killed by Opitz and his ilk; Harsdörffer and Morhof, for instance, found it possible later in the century to speak kindly of Hans Sachs, and Canitz went so far as to readopt the *Knittelvers*.[1] Yet it was branded by the Opitzianer as inferior, or at best patronisingly as "altdeutsch". The change in literary standards and methods reflected in some measure the change in society. The *Meistergesang* was the highly characteristic expression of the craftsman class in a century when the burgher was the stoutest pillar of society. In the seventeenth century, the age of princely absolutism, German literature underwent a re-orientation to become oligarchic and aristocratic. As far as verse was concerned, the new 'respectable' literature, the *Kunstdichtung*, was founded on the alexandrine. *Knittelverse* continued to be used, but mainly as occasional verses composed for festive occasions such as betrothals and weddings. As it happened, the *Meistergesang* was henceforth virtually identified by the pundits with the doggerel of the *Pritschmeister*, who since the late Middle Ages had been present at all the shooting festivals organised by well-to-do burghers.[2] His function was partly that of master of cere-monies, and partly of entertainer; that is, he was required to keep order, control the course of the programme, and amuse the spectators. The symbol of his authority was the *Pritsche* which he used when demanding silence and punishing offenders. When called upon, he had to declaim doggerel verse appropriate to the occasion, that is in praise of those who had promoted the festival, and to ridicule the less skilled marksmen. In the heyday of the burgher the *Pritschmeister* was a respected member of society. As the position of his patron declined in the seventeenth century, his own status and moral authority deteriorated. Where the burgher festivals continued to take place, his rôle was that of buffoon, and his *Pritsche* identified with the harlequin's staff. But he remained a familiar figure during Gryph's lifetime and indeed for some time after-wards. The *Pritschmeister's* lines were invariably *Knittelverse*. This metre was regarded by the representatives of the new poetry as quaint and antiquated, and consequently became the butt of satirical writings.[3] *Peter Squentz* can claim to be the most distinguished of these. The third act contains a delightful burlesque of the old style. The metre is traditional with an occasional outrageous line (by way of an ungentle

[1] Cp. O. Flohr: Geschichte des Knittelverses, etc. (*Berliner Beiträge zur germ. & roman. Philol.*, Germ. Abt. No. 1).

[2] Cp. K. Bachler: *Der Pritschmeister Wolfgang Ferber der Altere* (1586–1657). Diss. Breslau, 1929.

[3] It should be remembered that in sixteenth-century Germany the habit of rhyming was universal, from prince to peasant, priest to prostitute, and that textbooks on every subject appeared in rhymed doggerel.

prod); the rhyme is both masculine and feminine, with assonances here and there; the style is ungainly, the vocabulary uninspired and even uncouth, the sequence of thoughts frequently faulty and obviously dependent on the rhyme; apocope and syncope occur, and the attributive adjective occasionally follows the noun—features proscribed by seventeenth-century grammarians.

Although by 1600 its heyday had passed, the *Meistergesang*, like the *Pritschmeisterei*, lived on into the next century and in some areas into the eighteenth. Moreover it was firmly established in Breslau and Görlitz, the region in which the *Kunstpoesie* was born. *Peter Squentz*, then, not only bears witness to the literary revolution, it was composed in the middle of it, and gave it a hearty push onward. Lollinger's song with its absurd text and ingenuous melody leaves us in no doubt about Gryph's target. We may be sure that the play amused his audience too: „Wenn fie beffer wären / würden wir fo fehr nicht brüber lachen" says the king of Squentz's miserable lines. Gryph's acquaintance with Sachs' dramas is recorded in *Peter Squentz*. At the beginning of the second act[1] the marshal reads Squentz's repertory and it transpires that, apart from *Piramus und Thisbe*, there are eleven in all (compared with three in *A Midsummer Night's Dream*). Nine of these show an unmistakable resemblance to plays of Sachs; as for *Susanna*, this was the most commonplace of themes in sixteenth-century drama. In other words, in Gryph's comedy the plays of Sachs constitute by far the major part of the repertory of this band of ignorant craftsmen. The fact that, as it turns out, they cannot perform any of them is immaterial; what is important is that they are the kind of play Squentz and his crew would want to produce if they could.

If it was Gryph's purpose to discredit certain of the 'popular' writers, he did it good-humouredly. Nowhere in this burlesque is there a vicious attack as on a hated adversary; on the contrary, we can imagine Gryphius chuckling to himself as he wrote the little sketch. Especially Bullabutäin's monologue in the third act must have given him keen pleasure. Here at the end of every alternate line he substitutes a synonym for the rhyming word, the result being execrable rhymeless doggerel.[2] The target of the satire is really twofold; in addition to the 'popular' literature there is the incompetence and pretentiousness of dilettanti who are not nearly equal to their self-appointed tasks. The latter, because it is omnipresent and perennial, has the wider and more permanent appeal. The satire on the former will have been savoured rather more fully by an educated seventeenth-century audience with direct experience of the *Meistergesang*, *Schwänke*, the *Pritschmeister*, and

[1] Cp. Commentary.
[2] Cp. Commentary.

4

of the controversy concerning them. This particular aspect of the burlesque was certainly more exciting for Gryph's contemporaries than for us today, however vividly we may be able to picture the revolution in literary taste.

D. PETER SQUENTZ AND THE QUINCE EPISODE IN
A Midsummer Night's Dream

AS it is very doubtful whether Gryphius ever knew *A Midsummer Night's Dream*, we should be careful not to base an appraisal of Gryph's achievement on Shakespeare's play or even on the yokel scenes in it. It is obvious that a connection exists between the two works, and a comparison is interesting, but the aim and intention of the authors were by no means identical. In his preface Gryphius tells us that he had arranged for *Peter Squentz* to be performed along with one of his tragedies,[1] so that it was from the first probably designed to provide comic relief after tragic scenes. Now in Gryph's tragedies the action is almost negligible and the pattern of the plot insignificant. The characterisation of the main figures is weak; the heroes are ethereal beings, and the villains mere foils to them. The poet's principal achievement lies in the language. *Peter Squentz*, unlike the clownery of Quince and his crew in Shakespeare's work, is an independent play. There is no atmosphere of fairies, gossamer, and magic to influence the behaviour of these simple folk. Their actions make nonsense, the plot is farcical, but the language again is important. The characters are grotesque—even more so to us today—and their bearing provoked the audience to hearty laughter. No subtle humour, but boisterous, down-to-earth fun.

The satire on literary fashions discussed above was not an innovation in Gryph's comedy as compared with the mechanicals' play in Shakespeare's work. It is true that the larger number of verse lines in the *Dream* is rhymed; but side by side with these, and especially with the ease and polish of the blank verse, the metre in the English Piramus play is a primitive jig—a satire, it is generally accepted, on the rhyming mother wits whose style was characterised to some extent by omission of the definite and indefinite articles and, like the *Knittelvers*, by apocope and syncope.[2] Squentz introduces his play with a prologue (much

---

[1] Probably *Cardenio und Celinde*.

[2] Cp. *Cambises* and *Sir Clyomon and Sir Clamides*. The first (and most serious) part of Thomas Preston's *Cambises* is in rhymed couplets, each line being of seven feet, a metre common at the time; but in the second (comic) part the verse is of four accented syllables, the number of syllables to a line being irregular.

longer than Quince's) in which he gives an outline of the plot. This was in the tradition of the old Moralities and Shrovetide plays which still lingered on in the seventeenth century, and here Gryphius is making fun of this old practice. In Shakespeare's play the introductory speech together with the later explanatory 'asides' by Wall, Moonshine, and Lion match in length the play proper. His butt, too, was the prologues, presenters, and dumbshows in the older dramas where the authors had not the technical skill to convey the information by means of dialogue. Then there is the satire on the strata of society (preserved in some measure at least in the German version), from the lords and ladies, through jester and butler, to Bottom and the fairies.

Like Gryphius, Shakespeare has his sport good-humouredly; his is no "serpent's tongue" in this play. Benedetto Croce expressed himself poetically but shrewdly when he remarked that the *Dream* "seems born of a smile."[1] Gryph's sketch "batters at the judicious ribs," to use Lamb's phrase. Neumeister, a younger contemporary of Gryphius, wrote of it: "Peter Squentz makes everybody's sides split with laughing."[2] The farcical antics of Squentz and his men are indeed rather more boisterous than the complacent and ingenuous nonsense of the English mechanicals. „Jch habe gelacht / daß mir die Augen übergehen" gasps the queen at the end. On the other hand, when Shakespeare's queen Hippolyta protests: "This is the silliest stuff that ever I heard," Theseus makes the exquisite reply: "The best in this kind are but shadows: and the worst are no worse, if imagination amend them"—a delicacy of humour we should seek in vain in Gryph's drama and probably elsewhere in seventeenth-century German literature. The corresponding line in *Squentz* comes when Serenus comments ironically on the schoolmaster's doggerel, and Theodoru answers „Wenn fie beffer wären / würden wir fo fehr nicht drüber lachen."

When the Quince episode was torn from its setting, as I believe it was, taken to Holland and Germany, and performed at court, in street, and market place by the English Comedians, it was natural that it should coarsen. We have no direct evidence of the quality of the various German adaptations that grew out of the material, but there are a number of the plays of the itinerant actors still extant, and judging from these it is probable that Gryph's play was a deal more refined than those of the *Wanderbühne*. Once taken out of the dream play, it necessarily changed in character. This was what happened when Shakespeare's drama was cut down to the Piramus play in England. The

---

[1] *Ariosto, Shakespeare, and Corneille*, trans. D. Ainslee, p. 172.

[2] Erdmann Neumeister: *Dissertatio historico-critica de poëtis Germanicis hujus seculi praecipius*, Lipsiae, 1695.

charm of the poetry had vanished, the music faded out, the magic dispelled, the atmosphere of mystery and fantasy evaporated. The only moonlight left was Moonshine. Thus it was with Gryph's comedy. The preparations of the mechanicals for their performance had now to be extended, as this was to be a play in its own right. Once it was wrenched from its context, the rôle of Bottom naturally lost its importance, for in the original Bottom's love-affair with Titania was a vital link with the dream play, and he himself a favourite character of Shakespeare.

Changed though the atmosphere, tone, and character of the play may be, the players in the German sketch are still craftsmen. The carpenter, weaver, bellowsmender, tinker, tailor, and joiner are there, but the rôles have been changed. Squentz is no longer a carpenter but a clerk and village schoolmaster. Bulla Butäin (Bully Bottom) is the bellowsmender, Kricks the tinker, Klotz-George serves the tailor, Klipperling is the joiner, and the weaver Lollinger. The carpenter seems to be merged with the joiner. Pickelhäring as court jester is a significant addition to the players which will be discussed later. Shakespeare's choice of names for Bottom and his fellows, inasmuch as they are indicative of their several crafts, is not lost sight of in the German play. Bottom[1] meant the core of a skein of yarn, Snout was the nozzle or spout; Starveling was apt, for "it takes nine tailors to make a man", as the saying went. Quince came from "quines" or "quoins", i.e. a wedge of wood or stone used in building. Snug was of course close-fitting, whilst Flute reminds us of the church organ which had its bellows. . . . In Gryph's play Bulla Butäin is a corruption of Bully Bottom; Klipperling was a form of mallet. "Klotz" in Klotz-George is not so obvious, but it may have signified the unhewn wood from which the spool was fashioned, or it could be an echo of the "quoin" just mentioned.[2] The name Lollinger seems to have had a historical basis.[3] Kricks is obscure, unless it is intended to be imitative of one of the sounds made by the tinker at work; an alternative explanation might be that he is supposed to be captious and quarrelsome (kricklich). Gryph's innovations[4] are the new profession given to Squentz, the additional accomplishment of mastersinger to the weaver, the casting of the fountain as a live character, and Pickelhäring—all having a satirical function. Instead of the wedding of Theseus and Hippolyta the

---

[1] In the Schlegel-Tieck translation "Bottom" is rendered as "Zettel", i.e. "warp".

[2] In Silesia and the Austro-Bavarian region the Christian name was sometimes put after the surname. Cp. Laube's novel *Der Schatten Wilhelm*.

[3] Cp. p. xlvii above.

[4] Cp. his preface.

occasion for the performance is an evening's relaxation after a meeting of the *Reichstag*.

Pickelhäring is a very subdued jester, we might say, when compared with some of his namesakes in the plays of the *Wanderbühne*, but he still has certain of the tricks and mannerisms which had made this clown so celebrated a figure throughout Germany. He occasionally steps out of his part to address the audience directly; he continues clowning when he is supposed to be a lifeless corpse; he makes the most frightful grimaces when feigning a death agony; he permits himself an indecent remark here and there, and his repartee is sometimes made to rhyme with his companion's line. It is clear too, that Gryphius recognised the importance of this rôle—an importance it had acquired since the arrival in Germany of the itinerant English players. Squentz as producer allots the part of Piramus to "Juncker Pickelhäring", i.e. the most exalted person in the comedy is played by the most distinguished member of the cast, for Pickelhäring after all is "des Königs lustiger Rath." Gryph's jester, moreover, is jealous of his identity and prefers not to be associated with "Jehan Potage"—a kind of clown who, in the past and apparently without any real evidence, has been given a French origin. The German form of the name as it appeared at the time is "Hans Supp(e)", and the name "Jean Potage" did not feature in the plays of the Englishmen. Pickelhäring, on the other hand, was considered by Gryph's contemporaries as a figure imported from across the Channel:

> „Diesen Monsieur Pickelhäring haben die Engländischen erstmalen in Deutschland eingeführet / da es noch in guten Wohlstand war / und jedermann gerne mit Comödien und anderen Aufzügen sich belustiget / welches nicht mehr viel geschehen wird."[1]

On the title-page of the 1620 edition of *Engelische Comedien und Tragedien*[2] the name "Pickelhering" is given prominence in the centre; he was, then, a considerable attraction. Some of the more successful of the English actors created their own fashion in clowns, e.g. at the end of the sixteenth century Thomas Sackville became known in Wolfenbüttel and elsewhere for his "John Bouset", John Spencer for his "Hans Stockfisch", Robert Reynolds for his "Robert Pickelhäring"—names which caught the imagination of the public more firmly than Heinrich Julius' "Johan Clant" and Ayrer's "Jahn Clam". It seems probable that in their efforts to preserve some measure of individuality for their

---

[1] *Illuminirter Reichs und Welt-Spiegel* (1631). Cp. Cohn, *op. cit.*, p. xcviii, and Creizenach: *Die Schauspiele der englischen Komödianten*, p. xcv.

[2] Reproduced in Tittmann's *Die Schauspiele der englischen Komödianten in Deutschland*, p. 1.

own creatures, these actors adopted distinctive features in their dress. Thus we have a description of Pickelhäring and Jean Potage as they appeared on the title-page of a political pamphlet[1] in Gryph's own day. The phrase "Englischer Pickelhäring" was current in seventeenth-century Germany, and apart from suggesting the origin of this kind of clown, the adjective indicates the popularity of the English actors.[2]

Returning to Gryph's Pickelhäring, he is admittedly subdued, but we do get a sample of the antics which made the German audiences shake with laughter. When Thisbe discovers her lover lying "dead" and stoops to kiss him, Piramus (Pickelhäring) „ſchnappet nach ihr mit dem Maul"; and he continues to speak to Thisbe after he has "died". His display of fisticuffs, unbecoming as it is in a nobleman, does not occur in Shakespeare's play. Indeed, whereas in the German version the Piramus play is repeatedly interrupted by knockabout farce, and ends with the "dead" Piramus carrying off his lady on his shoulders, in Shakespeare's episode the ingenuousness, gentle pathos, and melancholy gaiety persist to the end. Pickelhäring insists that he has no memory for lines and finds Latin difficult. He makes himself out to be so illiterate that we wonder how he came by the appointment of court jester; but then occasionally he surprises us with tit-bits of knowledge, e.g. the landmarks in Danzig and Augsburg, and the reference to the nine muses and their origin as nymphs of wells and springs, so that we ask ourselves whether his ignorance was not feigned in order to fool his audience. Whatever Pickelhäring's legitimate claims to his profession as clown, Squentz himself gets more laughs, although these are apt to be at his own expense, viz. his counterfeit scholarship. His comedy is achieved mainly by word of mouth, Pickelhäring's by miming. In one context Squentz is identified with the Fool associated with the old Moralities, i.e. as presenter of the play.[3]

Gryph's *Peter Squentz* is one of the most successful plays of its kind in the German language, and certainly the most distinguished in the seventeenth century. A critical appreciation of the work should on no account be undertaken as if it were a direct adaptation of Shakespeare's *A Midsummer Night's Dream*. There was no question of emulating the English poet. Indeed, as we have seen, this and others of Shakespeare's plays were probably unknown to Gryphius. The circumstances were that Gryphius took over the script of a popular farce based on the

[1] Cp. Illustration opposite.

[2] I think it quite possible, too, that the name involved a pun with a distinctly ironical flavour, as "eng(e)lisch" meant "angelic" in the language of the time, and Pickelhäring was anything but that.

[3] Cp. p. xv above. The anonymous Piramus and Thisby play of 1581 and Damian Türckis' play on the same theme (circa 1607) both included a "Narr". Cp. p. xlii, n.2.

Pickelhering and Jean Potage

(From a seventeenth-century engraving. Cp. p. 41)

Bottom episode in *A Midsummer Night's Dream*, and turned it into a knockabout burlesque of contemporary German life. What the German writer set out to do here, he did well. To assert that *Squentz* has none of the poetic fancy that characterises the work of the world's greatest poet would be true, but it is irrelevant to an assessment of Gryph's achievement as author of this "absurda comica". It is neither devastating nor helpful criticism to say that *Squentz* is crude. It was intended to be precisely that.[1] Here and elsewhere in his work Gryph's comedy employs certain familiar expedients, viz. horseplay, comic miming, naturalistic use of language, direct speech with the spectators, and misunderstanding of foreign languages—devices which of course are familiar in the literature of other lands. The mechanicals' royal audience, moreover, entertains us with occasional flashes of wit. What we scarcely find in *Squentz*, and what appears to be rare in German drama altogether, is *humour*.[2]

E. EDITIONS AND PERFORMANCES OF THE PLAY

THERE has been some uncertainty about the date of composition of *Peter Squentz*, principally because the first two editions of the play bore no date, no author's name, no publisher's name, and no place of publication. It seems not unreasonable to relate the unusual

---

[1] As Gottsched remarked (cp. p. xli above) the material of the play was "auf deutschen Fuß eingerichtet." The reasons why this was what comedy in seventeenth-century Germany amounted to, are naturally interesting, but they constitute a wider field of study. Cp. pp. xxv *et seq.*

[2] Gundolf's criticism of *Peter Squentz* (*Shakespeare und der deutsche Geist*, pp. 75 *et seq.*) misses the mark, first of all because he fails to distinguish between humour and comedy. For him comedy which is not intellectual is inferior, and he condemns Gryph's play as a *Posse*, which after all it was intended to be; in other words he begs the question. "Gryphius," he says, "erscheint in Peter Squentz dagegen nicht als ein Mann der lachen will, sondern als einer der lachen machen will"—and yet whoever takes the trouble to read the play, will not only be greatly diverted but will also conclude that Gryphius must have enjoyed himself hugely *as he wrote it.* The following two quotations will, I think, illustrate the nature of Gundolf's criticism: "Verglichen mit der *Kunst über alle Künste* ist des Andreas Gryphius *Absurda Comica oder Peter Squentz*, die Bearbeitung der Rüpelkomödie aus dem Sommernachtstraum (ohne Kenntnis des Shakespeareschen Originals aber mit Kenntnis deutscher Theaterstücke) ein blosser Schwank." Later he continues: "Nun ist schon die ganze Art wie Gryphius die Fabel übernommen und umgestaltet hat ein Zeichen für seinen Mangel an eigentlich komischem Sinn," and he condemns Gryphius for taking the play out of the setting it had in *A Midsummer Night's Dream*. As there is no evidence that the Squentz material had ever been performed in Germany in its original setting, and as Gryphius mentions his source in his preface, Gundolf's criticism must be regarded as anything but circumspect.

circumstances of this publication to Gryph's reference (in his preface to
Horribilicribrifax) to „die Thorheiten feiner Jugend" and to explain it
by the author's diffidence at declaring himself publicly as a writer of
comedies. But this would not account satisfactorily for the absence of
the publisher's name. The explanation may be that the play was
printed as an appendix to the 1657 edition of the poetical works, thus
completing the 1658 edition.[1] In any case there was a delay in printing
both these comedies which were probably written between 1647 and
1649, that is during a period of leisure between his return from the
grand tour and his acceptance of the post of syndic.[2] Peter Squentz is a
witness to the marriage contract in *Horribilicribrifax* between Sempronius and Cyrilla which is dated 30 Feb. (*sic*) 1648. Braune[3] has
brought sound bibliographical and typographical evidence that *Squentz*
was first printed in 1657 and secondly in 1663.[4]

A posthumous edition of *Squentz* appeared in the 1698 publication of
Gryph's works supervised by his son Christian. It corrected misprints
in the previous editions, and also introduced minor textual variations.
Since that date the following have appeared:

1. *Herr Peter Squenz, in einem kurzweiligen Lust-Spiel vorgestellt.*
   Frankfurt, Bey Lorenz Felpüsch, 1750.

2. In the second volume of Tieck's *Deutsches Theater*, 1817.

3. In *Dramatische Dichtungen von A. Gryphius*, edited by J. Tittmann,
   1870.

4. In Reclams Universal-Bibliothek, Nr. 917, 1877. "Für die
   heutige Leserwelt herausgegeben von Karl Pannier." This bowdlerised version has recently been superseded by a complete edition
   by H. Cysarz in Reclams Universal-Bibliothek, Nr. 917, 1954.

5. In *Neudrucke*, Nr. 6, 1877. Abdruck der Ausgabe von 1663,
   herausgegeben W. Braune.

---

[1] The 1658 edition bears the title: *Andreae Gryphii Freuden und Trauer-Spiele
auch Oden und Sonnette sampt Herr Peter Squentz Schimpff-Spiel.*
[2] Cp. Gryph's preface to *Squentz*: „Weil er aber hernach als felbter mit
wichtigern Sachen bemühet / von ihm gantz in Vergessen gestellet."
[3] *Neudrucke*, No. 6, pp. iii *et seq.*
[4] The controversy concerning the date of origin and of the first two editions of
Squentz has been carried on by the following: Braune, *op. cit.*; Bredow, *Nachgelassene Schriften*, p. 106; J. Herrmann, *Über A. Gryphius* (Programm der städti-
schen Realschule zu Leipzig vom Jahr 1851); Koberstein-Bartsch, *Grundr. d.
Nat. Lit.*, Vol. II, p. 255; Manheimer, Gryphius-Bibliographie (*Euphorion*, Vol.
XI); Palm, *Lustspiele, & DNL*, No. 29, pp. 194 *et seq.*; Tieck, *Deutsches Theater*,
Vol. II; Tittmann, *Dramatische Dichtungen von A. Gryphius*; Wentzlaff-Eggebert,
Bibliographie der Gryphius-Drucke in *Andreas Gryphius Lateinische und deutsche
Jugenddichtungen*.

6. In *Andreas Gryphius Lustspiele*, herausgegeben Hermann Palm (Lit. Verein, Stuttgart, Nr. CXXXVIII, 1878). This is based on the posthumous edition of 1698.
7. *Absurda Comica oder Herr Peter Squenz.* Edited with introduction, notes, and exercises by Sydney H. Moore, 1908. This is a bowdlerised edition based on Pannier's.
8. In 1924 in Berlin a limited edition (600 copies) of a reprint of the 1663 edition was published with original woodcuts by Max Unold.
9. A second edition of No. 5 above was prepared by H. Becker and published in 1955.

Bredow's free adaptation of Gryph's play was published posthumously in *Nachgelassene Schriften* in 1816.

Information on the performances of Gryph's play is very meagre. In his preface the poet mentions that he had arranged for it to be performed with one of his tragedies, but he gives no further details. It is probable that the production in Dresden on 20 February 1672, of *M. Peter Squenz Comoedia* was of Gryph's work,[1] and the performance in Torgau on 3 March 1680.[2] Once published, it was the most accessible form of a Squentz-play and doubtless in great demand with itinerant actors. In 1682 appeared Christian Weise's *Lustiges Nachspiel, wie etwan vor diesem von Peter Squentz aufgeführet worden, von Tobias und der Schwalbe*—an adaptation of the Squenz theme in which the poet abandoned the Piramus and Thisbe play, span the work out to four acts, and added a moral. It is by no means as attractive a comedy as Gryph's.[3]

We do not know definitely on which sort of stage *Peter Squentz* was produced in Gryph's day; that is whether it was a simple stage with a front curtain, or one divided into two parts by an inner curtain. The latter variety which also had a front curtain, was used for his tragedies.[4] The presentation of a play within the play in the third act of *Peter Squentz* certainly suggests the *zweiteilige Bühne* as the more suitable.[5]

[1] Cp. M. Fürstenau, *op. cit.*, erster Teil, p. 235.

[2] Cp. M. Hammitzsch: *Der höfische Theaterbau* (*Der moderne Theaterbau*, erster Teil, p. 116).

[3] Later echoes of the play are dealt with by A. v. Weilen in Aus dem Nachleben des Peter Squenz und des Faustspiels (*Euphorion*, Vol. II), and by E. Schmidt in Aus dem Nachleben des Peter Squentz (*Zs. f. dt. Altert.*, Vol. XXVI). "Peter Squenz" seems to have survived for a long time as a symbolic name for a charlatan, as for example in the adaptation of Molière's *Le médecin malgré lui*, published in Frankfurt am Main in 1776 under the title of *Peter Squenz oder die Welt will betrogen seyn*.

[4] Cp. the illustrations facing p. cxxix in my edition of *Carolus Stuardus*. The following suggestions are in agreement with those of W. Flemming in *A. Gryphius und die Bühne*, pp. 319 et seq.

[5] The stage Gryphius had in mind for *Horribilicribrifax* was certainly partitioned by an inner curtain, viz.: Cleander: Jch bitte / fie treten etwas hinter die Tapete unb hören unferen Reben mit Gebult zu! (Act V, Sc. 2).

If then we imagine a production on such a stage, the positioning of the characters will have probably been something like this: at the beginning of the play the front curtain is drawn back to reveal the mechanicals already assembled front stage, perhaps in a semi-circle, for Squentz immediately calls the roll. The background is provided by the inner curtain which conceals the inner stage, as this is a room of modest proportions in a tavern or Squentz's own home. The inner curtain, it should be remembered, was often painted in Gryph's day to form part of the set. There are no comings or goings in the first act, except at the end, and as there is an important piece of comic miming with Squentz and Pickelhäring at the exit, this was no doubt front stage.

The front curtain is drawn at the end of the first act, and at the beginning of the second reveals a room in the palace. This act might well require the whole stage, since although only six persons are mentioned, there will be others also in attendance; e.g. in the third act a "Hofediener" (not mentioned otherwise) pushes Squentz's stool from under him.

In the last act, however, there is no doubt that the whole stage is in use, for not only are we told that "die Personen alle" are present, but the players' sketch is set back stage. The king and queen sit front stage, possibly to the left. The prince and princess may be at their side, or may sit opposite, front stage right, but in either case etiquette demands that the players should enter facing the king. There will of course be another doorway on the opposite side of the stage, and both of them will be well back. Grouped behind the king and queen are the remaining courtiers, and if the prince and princess sit opposite, on their side a couple of attendants of whom one plays the trick on Squentz. The latter, as producer of the Piramus and Thisbe play, sits on his stool diagonally opposite the king further back stage—near enough to the mechanicals to become involved in the brawl later.

F. BIBLIOGRAPHICAL NOTE

PETER SQUENTZ appeared twice in Gryph's lifetime. On the second occasion the text was bound with the 1663 edition of the poetical works, and it is on this printing that the present edition is based:

Andreae Gryphii | Freuden | und | Trauer=Spiele | auch | Oden | und | Sonnette. | In Breßlau zu finden | Bey | Veit Jacob Treſ= chern / Buchhändl. | [Rule] | Leipzig / | Gedruckt bey Johann Erich Hahn. | Im Jahr 1663. |

This volume has continuous pagination to p. 777, which includes the tragedies, the Freudenspiel *Majuma*, the *Kirchhoffs-Gedancken*, four books of odes, and four of sonnets. The remainder of the volume, consisting of the comedies, epigrams, and the *Weicherstein*, has distinct pagination, and was published for the most part, if not all, by Jacob Drescher. The separate items are apt to be bound in different sequence in different copies.[1]

Format: 8vo. $A^{1a}-C^{7b}$. Pp. [4] 1–42 [2].

The letterpress covers 36 lines + headline and signature and catchword line. 126 (135) × 85 mm. Size of page = 160 × 100 mm.

A^{1a}	title
A^{1b}	blank
$A^{2a}-A^{2b}$	preface
A^{3a}	dramatis personae
$A^{3b}-C^{7b}$	text

A^{1a} = Abſurda Comica. | Oder | Herr Peter Squentz / | Schimpff=Spiel.

[1] I used the British Museum copy.

Abfurda Comica.

Oder

Herr Peter Squentz/
Schimpff-Spiel.

.

Großgünstiger Hochgeehrter Leser.

DEr nunmehr in Deutſchland nicht unbekante, und ſeiner Meynung nach Hochberühmbte[1] Herr Peter Squentz wird dir hiermit über= geben. Ob ſeine Anſchläge gleich nicht alle ſo ſpitzig / als er ſich ſelber düncken läſt / ſind doch ſelbte bißher auff unterſchiedenen Schau= plätzen nicht ohne ſondere Beliebung und Erluſtigung der Zuſeher angenommen und belachet worden: Warumb denn hier und dar Gemütter gefunden / welche ſich vor gar ſeinen Vater auszugeben weder Scheu noch Bedencken getragen. Worinnen er weit glückſeliger geweſen / alſo nicht wenig Kinder dieſer Zeit / die auch leibliche Eltern / wenn ſie vornehmlich etwas zu frühe ankommen / vor die ihrigen nicht erkennen wollen: Damit er aber nicht länger Frembden ſeinen Vrſprung zu dancken habe / ſo wiſſe; Daß der umb gantz Deutſchland wolverdienete / und in allerhand Sprachen und Mathe= matiſchen Wiſſenſchafften ausgeübete Mann / Daniel Schwenter[2]/ ſelbigen zum erſten zu Altdorff auff den Schauplatz geführet / von dannen er je länger je weiter gezogen / biß er endlich meinem liebſten Freunde begegnet / welcher ihn beſſer ausgerüſtet / mit neuen Per= ſonen vermehret / und nebens einem ſeiner Traurſpiele aller Augen und Vrtheil vorſtellen laſſen.[3] Weil er aber hernach / als ſelbter mit wichtigern Sachen bemühet / von ihm gantz in Vergeſſen geſtellet:[4] Habe ich mich erkühnet / ihn Herrn Peter Squentz aus gedachten meines Freundes Bibliothec abzufordern / und durch öffentlichen Druck dir / (Großgünſtiger und Hochgeehrter Leſer / zu überſenden / wirſt du ihn mit deiner Begnügung auffnehmen / ſo erwarte mit ehiſtem den unvergleichlichen Horribilicribrifan, von deſſen Pinſel abgemahlet / dem Herr Peter Squentz die letzte Strüche ſeiner Voll= kommenheit zu dancken / und bleib hiermit gewogen deinem ſtets Dienſt ergebenen

Philip-Gregorio Rieſentod.

Spielende Perfonen.[5]

Herr Peter Squentz / Schreiber und Schulmeister zu Rumpels=
Kirchen / Prologus und Epilogus.
Pickelhäring / des Königes luftiger Rath / Piramus.
Meister Krix / über und über / Schmied / der Monde.
Meister Bulla Butäin / Blasebalckmacher / die Wand.
Meister Klipperling / Tischler / der Löwe.
Meister Lollinger Leinweber und Meister Sänger / der Brunn.
Meister Klotz=George / Spulenmacher / Thisbe.

Zusehende Perfonen.

Theodorus, der König.

Serenus, der Printz.

Cassandra, die Königin.

Violandra, Princeßin.

Eubulus, der Marschalck.

Abſurda Comica.

oder

Herr Peter Squentz.

Erſter Auffzug.

Peter Squentz, **Pickelhäring / Meiſter Kricks über und über / Meiſter** Bulla-Butän **Meiſter Klipperling / Meiſter Lollinger / Meiſter Klotz-George.**

P. Squentz.

Edler / Woledler / Hochedler / Woledelgeborner Herr Pickel= häring / von Pickelhäringsheim und Saltznaſen.

Pickelh. Der bin ich.[6]

P. Sq. Arbeitſamer und Armmächtiger Meſter Kricks / über und über / Schmied.

M. Kricks über. Der bin ich.

P. Sq. Tugendſamer / auffgeblaſener und windbrechender Meſter Bullabutän / Blaſebalckenmacher.

Bullabutän. Der bin ich.

P. Sq. Ehrwürdiger / durchſchneidender und gleichmachender Meſ= ter Klipperling / Wollbeſtellter Schreiner des weitberühmbten Dorffes / Rumpels=Kirchen.

M. Klipperl. Der bin ich.

P. Sq. Wolgelahrter / vielgeſchwinder und hellſtimmiger Meſter Lollinger / Leinweber und Meſter Sänger.

Loll. Der bin ich.

P. Sq. Treufleiſſiger / Wolwürckender / Tuchhaffter[7] Meſter Klotz= George / Spulenmacher.

M. Klotz=George. Der bin ich.

P. Sq. Verſchraubet euch[8] durch Zuthuung euer Füſſe und Niederlaſſung der hinderſten Oberſchenckel auff herumbgeſetzte Stühle / ſchlüſſet die Repoſitoria euers Gehirnes auff / ver= ſchliſſet die Mäuler mit dem Schloß des Stillſchweigens / ſetzt eure 7. Sinnen[9] in die Falten / Herr Peter Squentz (cum titulis plenisſimis) hat etwas nachdenckliches anzumelden.

P. H. Ja / ja / Herr Peter Squentz iſt ein Tieffſinniger Mann / er hat einen Anſchlägigen Kopff /[10] wenn er die Treppen hinunter fällt / er hat ſo einen anſehnlichen Bart / als wenn er König von

Neu=Zembla[11] wäre / es ist nur zu bejammern / daß es nicht
wahr ist.[12]

P. Sq. Nach dem ich zweiffels ohn durch Zuthuung der alten
Phæbusſin[13] und ihrer Tochter der großmäulichen Frau Fama[13]
Bericht erlanget / daß Jhr Majeſt. unſer Geſtrenger Juncker
König ein groſſer Liebhaber von allerley luſtigen Tragœdien und
prächtigen Comœdien[14] ſey / als bin ich willens / durch Zuthuung
euer Geſchicligkeit eine jämmerlich ſchöne Comœdi zu tragiren /
in Hoffnung nicht nur Ehre und Ruhm einzulegen / ſondern auch
eine gute Verehrung für uns alle und mich ſpecie zuerhalten.

B. b. Das iſt erſchrecklich wacker! ich ſpiele mit / und ſolte ich 6.
Wochen nicht arbeiten.

P. H. Es wird über alle maſſen ſchöne ſtehen! wer wolte nicht
ſagen / daß unſer König treffliche Leute in ſeinem Dorffe hätte.

M. K. über und über. Was wollen wir aber vor eine tröſtliche
Comœdi tragiren?

P. Sq. Von Piramus und Thisbe.

M. Kl. G. Das iſt übermaſſen trefflich! man kan allerhand ſchöne
Lehre / Troſt und Vermahnung drauß nehmen / aber das ärgeſte
iſt / ich weiß die Hiſtorie noch nicht /[15] geliebt es nicht E. Herrligkeit dieſelbte zu erzehlen.

P. Sq. Gar gerne. Der Heil. alte Kirchen=Lehrer[16] Ovidius ſchrei-
bet in ſeinem ſchönen Buch Memoriumphoſis, das Piramus die
Thisbe zu einem Brunnen beſtellet habe / in mittelſt ſey ein abſcheu-
licher heßlicher Löwe kommen / vor welchem ſie aus Furcht ent-
lauffen / und ihren Mantel hinterlaſſen / darauff der Löwe Jungen
außgehecket; als er aber weggegangen / findet Piramus die bluttige
Schaube / und meinet der Löwe habe Thisben gefreſſen / darumb
erſticht er ſich aus Verzweiffelung / Thisbe kommet wieder und
findet Piramum todt / derowegen erſticht ſie ſich ihm zu Troß.[17]

P. H. Vnd ſtirbet?

P. Sq. Vnd ſtirbet.

P. H. Das iſt tröſtlich / es wird übermaſſen ſchön zu ſehen ſeyn:
aber ſaget Herr P. Sq. Hat der Löwe auch viel zu reden? **P. Sq.**
Nein / der Löwe muß nur brüllen. **P. H.** Ey ſo wil ich der Löwe
ſeyn / denn ich lerne nicht gerne viel außwendig.[18] **P. Sq.** Ey
Nein! Monſ. Pickelhering muß ein Hauptperſon agiren.[19] **P. H.**
Habe ich denn Kopff genug zu einer Hauptperſon?[20] **P. Sq.** Ja
freylich. Weil aber vornemlich ein tapfferer[21] ernſthaffter und
anſehnlicher Mann erfordert wird zum Prologo[22] und Epilogo, ſo
wil ich dieſelbe auff mich nehmen / und der Vorreder und Nach-
reder des Spiles / das iſt Anfang und das Ende ſeyn.

M. Kr. über und über. Jn Warheit. Denn weil ihr das Spiel macht / so ist billich / daß ihr auch den Anfang und das Ende dran setzet. M. Klip. Wer sol denn den Löwen nu tragiren? Ich halte er stünde mir am besten an / weil er nicht viel zu reden hat. M. Kricks. Ja mich düncket aber / es solte zu schrecklich lauten / wenn ein grimmiger Löwe hereingesprungen käme / und gar kein Wort sagte / das Frauenzimmer würde sich zu hefftig entsetzen. M. Klotz=G. Ich halte es auch dafür. Son=derlich wäre rathsam wegen Schwangerer Weiber/[23] daß ihr nur bald anfänglich sagtet / ihr wäret kein rechter Löwe / sondern nur Meister Klipperl. der Schreiner.

P. H. Vnd zum Wahr=Zeichen lasset das Schurtzfehl durch die Löwen Haut hervor schlenckern.

M. Loll. Wie bringen wir aber die Löwenhaut zu wege? Ich habe mein lebtage hören sagen / ein Löwe sehe nicht viel anders aus als eine Katze. Wäre es nun rathsam / daß man so vil Katzen schinden liesse / und überzüge euch nackend mit den noch bluttigen Fellen / daß sie desto fester anklebeten?

M. Kr. über und über. Eben recht. Es wäre ein schöner Handel / sind wir nicht mehrentheils Zunfftmässige Leute?[24] würden wir nicht wegen des Katzenschindens unredlich werden?

M. B. B. Es ist nicht anders. Darzu habe ich gesehen / daß die Löwen alle gelbe gemachet werden / aber meine lebetage keine gelbe Katze gefunden.

P. Sq. Ich habe einen andern Einfall. Wir werden doch die Comœdi bey Lichte tragiren. Nun hat mich mein Gevatter Mester Ditloff Ochsen=Fuß / welcher unser Rathhauß gemahlet / vor diesem berichtet / daß Grüne bey Lichte gelbe scheine. Mein Weib aber hat einen alten Rock von Früß/[25] den wil ich euch an stat einer Löwenhaut umbbinden.

M. Kr. Das ist das beste so zuerdencken / nur er muß der Rede nicht vergessen.

M. Kl. G. Kümmert euch nicht darumb liber Schwager / Herr Peter Squentz ist ein gescheidener[26] Mann / er wird dem Löwen wol zu reden machen.

Mester Klipperl. Kümmert euch nicht / kümmert euch nicht ich wil so lieblich brüllen / daß der König und die Königin sagen sollen / mein liebes Löwichen brülle noch einmal.

M. P. Sq. Lasset euch unterdessen die Nägel fein lang wachsen / und den Bart nicht abscheren / so sehet ihr einem Löwen desto ehnlicher / nun ist einer difficultet abgeholffen / aber hier wil mir das Wasser des Verstandes schier die Mühlräder des Gehirnes nicht mehr treiben / der Kirchen=Lehrer[27] Ovidius schreibet / daß der Monden geschienen habe / nun wissen wir nicht / ob der

Monde auch scheinen werde / wenn wir das Spiel tragiren
werden.

P. H. Das ist / beym Element / eine schwere Sache.[28]

M. Kricks. Dem ist leicht zu helffen / wir müssen im Calender[29]
sehen / ob der Monde denselben Tag scheinen wird.

M. Kl. G. Ja wenn wir nur einen hätten.

M. Loll. Hier habe ich einen / den habe ich von meines Groß=
Vatern Muhme ererbet / er ist wol 100. Jahr alt / und dero=
wegen schier der beste. Ey Juncker Pickelh. verstehet ihr euch
auffs Calendermachen / so sehet doch ob der Monde scheinen
wird.

P. H. Je solte ich daß nicht können / Lustig / lustig ihr Herren / der
Mond wird gewiß scheinen / wenn wir spilen werden.

M. Kricks. Ja ich habe aber mein lebetag gehöret / wenn man schön
Wetter im Calender findet / so regnets.

M. Kl. G. Drumb haben unsere lieben Alten gesaget; du leugest
wie ein Calender=macher.

P. Sq. Ey das ist nichts / der Mond muß darbey seyn / wenn wir
die Comœdi spielen / sonst wird das Ding zu Wasser / das ist die
Comœdi wird zu nichte.

M. Kricks. Hört was mir eingefallen ist / ich wil mir einen Pusch[30]
umb den Leib binden / und ein Licht in einer Latern tragen /
und den Monden tragiren, was düncket euch zu der Sachen.

P. H. Beym Velten[31] das wird gehen / aber der Monde muß in
der Höhe stehen. Wie hier zu rathen?

P. Sq. Es solte nicht übel abgehen / wenn man den Monden in
einen grossen Korb setzte / und denselben mit einem Stricke auff
und abliesse.

M. Kricks. Ja! wenn der Strick zuriesse / so fille ich herunter und
bräche Hals und Bein. Besser ist es / ich stecke die Laterne auff
eine halbe Picken /[32] daß das Licht umb etwas in die Höhe kommet.

P. Sq. Nec ita malè. Nur das Licht in der Laterne muß nicht zu
lang seyn / denn wenn sich Thisbe ersticht / muß der Mond seinen
Schein verlieren / das ist / verfinstert werden / und das muß
man abbilden mit Verleschung des Lichtes. Aber ad rem. Wie
werden wir es mit der Wand machen?

M. Klipperl. Ein Wand auffzubauen für dem Könige / das wird
sich nicht schicken.

P. H. Was haben wir viel mit der Wand zu thun?

P. Sq. Ey ja doch Piramus und Thisbe müssen mit einander durch
das Loch in der Wand reden.

M. Klipperl. Mich düncket / es wäre am besten / man beschmierete
einen umb und umb mit Leimwellern /[33] und steckte ihn auff die

Bühne / er müſte ſagen daß er die Wand wäre / wenn nun
Piramus reden ſoll / müſte er ihme zum Maule / das iſt zum
Loch hinein reden / Wenn nun Thisbe was ſagen wolte / müſte
er das Maul nach der Thisbe kehren.

P. Sq. Nihil ad Rhombum.[34] Das iſt: nichts zur Sache. Thisbe muß
dem Piramus den Liebespfeil durch das Loch ausziehen / wie
wollen wir das zu wege bringen?

P. H. Laſſet uns dennoch eine Papierne Wand machen / und ein
Loch dardurch bohren.

M. B. B. Ja / die Wand kan aber nicht reden.

M. Kricks. Das iſt auch wahr.

M. B. b. Ich wil mir eine Papierne Wand an einen Blindrähmen[35]
machen / und weil ich noch keine Perſon habe / ſo wil ich mit
der Wand auff den Platz kommen und ſagen / daß ich die Wand
ſey.

P. Sq. Appoſitè das wird ſich ſchicken / wie eine Härings=Naſen auff
einen Schwaben Ermel /[36] Juncker Pickelhäring ihr müſſet Piramus
ſeyn.

P. H. Birnen Moſt?[37] Was iſt das für ein Kerl.

P. Sq. Es iſt die vornemſte Perſon im Spiel / ein Chevalieùr
Soldat und Liebhaber.

M. Kl. G. Ja Pickelhäring iſt die fürnemſte Perſon im Spiel / er
muß das Spiel zieren / wie die Bratwurſt das Sauerkraut.[38]

P. H. Ein Soldat und Buler / ſo muß ich lachen und ſauer ſehen.

P. Sq. Aber nicht beydes auff einmahl.[39]

P. H. Das iſt gut! denn ich kan nicht zugleich lachen und weinen /
wie Jehan Potage. Es ſtehet auch einer ſo vornehmen Perſon /
wie ich bin / nicht an / ſondern iſt Närriſch[40] nicht Fürſtlich.
Nur ich bitte euch umb Gottes Willen / machet mir nicht viel
Lateiniſch in meinem Titul / die Wörter ſind mir zu Cauder=
welliſch / und wir verwirren das gantze Spiel. Denn ich weiß /
ich werde ſie nicht behalten.

P. Sq. Es wird ſich wol ſchicken. Ja nun wil mir das Hertze gar in
die Hoſen fallen.

M. Kl. G. Ey warumb Ehrenveſter Herr Peter Squentz.

P. Sq. Wir müſſen eine Thisbe haben / wo wollen wir die her
nehmen?

M. Loll. Das kan Klotz=George am beſten agiren, er hat als er
noch ein Knappe war / die Suſanna geſpielet / er machte ihm
die Augen mit Speichel naß / und ſah ſo barmhertzig[41] aus / daß
alle alte Weiber weinen muſten.

P. Sq. Ja und das gehet nun nicht an / er hat einen groſſen Bart.

P. H. Ohne Schaden: Er mag ihm das Maul[42] mit einem ſtücke.

Specke schmieren / so sihet er desto glätter aus umbs Mundstück /
und kan mit einer schmutzigen Goschen zum Fenster aus lucken.

M. Kricks. Freylich! nehmet die Personen an zu gutem Glück /
man weiß doch wol / daß ihr die rechte Thisbe nicht seyd.[43]

Bullabutäin. Ihr müsset fein klein / klein / klein reden.

M. Kl. G. Also?

P. Sq. Noch kleiner!

M. Kl. G. Also denn?

P. Sq. Noch kleiner.

M. Kl. G. Nun nun / ich wils wol machen / ich wil so klein und
lieblich reden / daß der König und Königin an mir den Narren
fressen sollen.

M. Loll. Was soll denn ich seyn?

P. Sq. Beim Element / wir hätten schir das nötigste vergessen /
ihr müsset der Brunnen seyn.

M. Loll. Was der Brunn?

P. Sq. Der Brunn.

M. Loll. Der Brunn? des muß ich lachen / ich bin ja einem Brunn
nicht ehnlich.

P. Sq. Ey ja verstehet eine Wasser=Kunst.[44]

P. H. Freylich / seyd ihr euer lebenlang nicht zu Dantzig gewesen /
oder zu Augspurg / die Maister=Sänger reisen[45] ja sonst zimlich
weit / habt ihr nicht gehöret / daß der Käyser zu Augspurg auff
einem Brunn stehet / und zu Dantzig Clinctunus..[46]

M. Loll. Aber wie sol ich Wasser von mir spritzen.

P. H. Seyd ihr so alt und wisset das nicht? ihr müsset vornen.[47]

P. Sq. Holla! Holla! Wir müssens Erbar machen für dem Frauen
Zimmer. Ihr müsset eine Gießkanne in der Hand haben.

P. H. Recht recht! so mahlet man das Wasser unter den 9. Freyen=
Künsten.[48]

P. Sq. Vnd must auch Wasser in dem Mund haben und mit umb
euch spritzen.

M. Kl. G. Wie wird er aber reden können?

P. Sq. Gar wol / wenn er einen Verß geredet hat / so muß er
einmal spritzen. Nun zu dem Titul dieses Spieles / wir sollen
es heissen eine Comœdi oder Tragœdie.

M. Loll. Der alte berühmbte deutsche Poët und Meister=Sänger
Hans Saxe[49] schreibet / wenn ein Spiel traurig ausgehet / so ist
es eine Tragœdie, weil sich nun hier 2. erstechen / so gehet es
traurig aus / Ergo.

P. H. Contra. Das Spiel wird lustig ausgehen / denn die Todten
werden wieder lebendig / setzen sich zusammen / und trincken
einen guten Rausch / so ist es denn eine Comœdie.

P. Sq. Ja es ist noch in weitem Feld. Wir wissen noch nicht ob wir
bestehen werden / vielleicht machen wir eine Sau und kriegen
gar nichts / darumm ist es am besten / ich folge meinem Kopff
und gebe ihm den Titul ein schön Spiel lustig und traurig / zu
tragiren und zu sehen.

M. Loll. Noch eines. Wenn wir das Spiel tragiren werden /
wollen wir dem Könige ein Register übergeben / darauff aller=
hand Comœdien verzeichnet / und diese zum letzten setzen / daß er
auslesen mag / was er sehen wil. Ich weiß / er wird doch keine
begehren als die letzte / unterdessen werden wir für geschickte und
hochgelehrte Leute gehalten werden.[50]

P. Sq. Gut gut! ihr Herren lernet fleissig / morgen mache ich die
Comœdi fertig / so kriget ihr die Zedel übermorgen / ich wil
unterdessen M. Lollingern den Meister=Sänger zu mir nehmen /
der wird mir schon helffen einrahten / wie ich die Endungen der
Syllben wol zusammen bringe / unter dessen seyd Gott befohlen.

P. H. Ehren / Wolehren und Hochehrenvester / tieffgelehrter / spitz=
findiger Herr P. Squentz grossen danck / eine gute Nacht.

Die andern nehmen alle mit allerhand Cerimo-
nien **von einander ihren Abscheid / Pickelhäring
aber und Peter Squentz nötigen einander
voranzugehen / so bald aber Squentz voran
tretten wil / zeucht ihn Pickelhäring zurück /
und laufft selbst voran.**

Der Ander Auffzug.

Theodorus. Caſſandra. Violandra. Serenus. Eubulus. P. Squentz.

Theodorus. Wir erfreuen uns höchst / das wir den nunmehr ver=
gangenen Reichs=Tag glücklich geendet / auch anwesende Abge=
sandten mit guter Vergnügung abgefertiget / mit was Kurtzweil
Herr Marschalck passiren wir vorstehenden Abend?

Eub. Durchläuchtigster König / es hat sich verwichene Tage ein
Seichtgelehrter Dorff=Schulmeister[51] nebens etlichen seines glei=
chen bey mir angemeldet / welcher willens vor ihrer Majestät
eine kurtzweilige Comœdi zu agiren, weil ich denn dieselbe sehr
annehmlich befunden /[52] in dem ich dem Versuch beygewohnet;

habe ich die gantze Gesellschafft auff diesen Abend herbeschieden /
und zweiffele nicht / ihre Majestät werden sich ob der guten Leute
Einfalt und wunderlichen Erfindungen nicht wenig erlustigen.

Cassandra. Wir sehen sehr gerne Comœdi und Tragœdien. Was
Inhalts des Spieles lassen sie anmelden.

Eub. Durchläuchtigste Princessin sie haben mir ein groß Register
voll überreichet / aus welchen Ihrer Majestäten frey stehet auß=
zulesen / was sie am angenehmsten düncket.

Seren. Leset uns doch die Verzeichnüß.[53]

Eub. Ein schön Spiel von der Verstörung Jerusalem.
Die Belägerung von Troja. Die Comœdia
von der Susanna. Die Com. von Sodom und
Gomorrha. Die Trag. von Ritter Petern mit
dem Silbernen Schlüssel. Vom Ritter Pontus.
Von der Melusina. Von Artus und dem Ostwind.
Von Carolus quinque. Die Comœdie von Julius
unus. Vom Hertzog und dem Teuffel / ein schön
Spiel lustig und traurig / kurtz und lang / schrecklich
und erfreulich. Von Piramus und Thisbe hat
hinten und forn nichts / niemals vor tragiret und
noch nie gedrucket / durch Peter Squentz Schul=
meistern daselbst.

Seren. Es scheinet die guten Schlucker können keine als die letzte /
darumb sie denn solche sonderlich außgestrichen / ruffet nur den
Principal selber herein / ich muß mich was mit ihm unterreden.

Eub. Durchläuchtigster Fürst / es ist ein schlechter[54] guter Mann /
er wird sich zweifels ohn entsetzen / und damit kommen wir umb
die Comœdi und verhoffte Lust.

Seren. Fodert ihn herein / wir wollen schon wissen mit ihm
umbzugehen.

Eub. Dieses ist die bewuste Person / Durchläuchtigster Fürst.

Seren. Seyd ihr der Author der Comœdi.

P. Sq. Ja mit züchten zu melden Juncker König.[55]

Theodor. Von wannen seyd ihr?

P. Sq. Tugendsamer Herr König ich bin ein Ober=Länder.[56]

Theodor. Wo habt ihr studiret?

P. Sq. Im Mägdeflecken auff der Neustad.

Theodor. Was habt ihr studiret.

P. Sq. Ich bin ein Universalem, das ist in allen Wissenschafften erfahren.

Theodor. Wo haltet ihr euch auff.

P. Sq. Vor diesem bin ich wolbestelter Glockenzieher des Spittel=glöckleins gewesen / weil ich mich aber über diese massen auff die Music des Glockengeklanges verstanden / bin ich nunmehr zu Rumpel=Kirchen wolbestelter Handlanger des Wortes Gottes / das ist Schreiber und Schulmeister auch Expectant des Pfarr=Ampts / wenn die andern alle werden gestorben seyn.[57]

Theodor. Seyd ihr denn auch tüchtig darzu?

P. Sq. Ja freylich /[58] in der gantzen Welt sind 4. Theil / Europa, Asia, Africa und America, unter diesen ist Europa das vor=nembste / in Europa sind unterschiedene Königreich / als Spa=nien / Portugall / Franckreich / Deutschland / Moschkau / En=gelland / Schottland / Dennemarck und Pohlen / unter allen aber ist Ober=Land das vornembste / weil es über Niederland / Oberland wird getheilet in Groß= und Klein=Oberland. Groß=Oberland hat den Vorzug / dannenhero heist es auch groß. In groß Ober=Land sind unterschiedene Creisser / als der Riesische / Gryllische / Würmische mit ihren vornehmsten Städten / als Fortzenheim / Narrenburg / Weißfischhausen / Kälberfurtz / Mägdeflecken. Diese letztere ist die trefflichste / denn die Mägd=lein oder Jungfern haben wieder den Vorzug / denn sie gehen voran. Zu Mägdeflecken gibt es unterschiedene Gassen / als die lange / die breite / die enge / die rechte / die krumme / die Roß=marien Gassen. Die Graupen=Gasse. Die Kerbe=Gasse. Die Lilien=Gasse / welche andere mit Verlaub aus Haß und Neyd die Dreck=Gasse nennen / unter allen ist die Lilien=Gasse die treff=lichste / denn auff derselben wohneten vor Zeiten viel vornehme gelehrte Leute / als Meister Girge Hackenbanck / Matz Stro=schneider / Meister Bulla=Butän / Meister Kricks über und über und Meister Klipperling / unter allen aber war ich der vornehmste. Ergò kan es nicht fehlen ich bin der vornehmste Mann in der gantzen Welt / das ist in Europa, Asia, Africa und America, ist niemand gleich.

Theodor. Wir nehmen mit höchster Verwunderung an / was ihr vorbringet / und erfreuen uns / daß wir so statliche und treff=liche Leute in unserm Lande haben.[59]

Seren. Aus so vielen Comœdien, die ihr zu agiren willens / begehren Ihre Majestät die erste zu sehen / von der Verstörung Jerusalem.

P. Sq. O potz tausend selten.[60]

Seren. Was sagt ihr darzu? nun wie stehet ihr so / was krümmert[61] ihr lange im Kopffe?

P. Sq. Die wolten wir wol tragiren, aber ihr müst uns zuvor Jerusalem lassen bauen / da wolten wir es zustören und einneh=men.

Seren. Wie stehets denn mit der Belägerung von Troja?

P. Sq. Es ist ein Ding.

Seren. Vnd was macht denn die schöne Susanna?

P. Sq. Wir wolten die wol tragiren, aber es würde übel stehen vor dem Frauen Zimmer / wann sich die Susanna nackend baden solte.

Seren. Was sagt ihr denn zu Sodom und Gomorrha?

P. Sq. Die wolten wir wol tragiren aber es würde viel Feuerwerck dazu gehören / wir möchten vielleicht den Teuffel gar anzünden.

Seren. Was sol man denn mit Rittern Peter machen?

P. Sq. Die wolten wir wol tragiren aber ihr müsset noch 14. Tage darauff harren.

Seren. Wie stehets denn mit Ritter Pontus?

P. Sq. Die wolten wir wol tragiren aber Ritter Pontus ist uns daraus gestorben.

Seren. Können wir die Melusinen sehen?

P. Sq. Das hat Meister Lollinger wider mein Wissen und Willen dazu gesetzet / den lasse ichs verantworten.

Seren. Sol denn Artus und der Ostwind mit einander fechten?[62]

P. Sq. Die wolten wir wol tragiren, aber der / der den Ostwind tragiret, ist itzt zu Schlieren Schlaff nach Wolle gezogen / könnet ihr geduld haben / biß er wieder komt / so wollen wir sehen / wie wir das Spiel zu wege bringen.

Seren. Was ist denn Carolus quinque vor einer gewesen?

P. Sq. Er ist seines Nahmens der Erste gewesen /[63] Julius unus der Andere / aber zu dem ersten mangeln uns die Kleider / und in der andern Comœdi ist zu viel Lateinisch. Es würde dem Gestren=gen Frauen=Zimmer nur verdrüßlich fallen.

Seren. Könnet ihr denn den Hertzog und den Teuffel einführen?

P. Sq. Das könten wir wol thun / aber es würde erschrecklich seyn / wenn der Teuffel kommen solte / die kleinen Kinder würden so drüber weinen / daß man sein eigen Wort nicht vernehmen könte.

Seren. Nun ich sehe / ihr seyd sehr wol ausgerüstet / es mangelt nun nichts mehr als die letzte von Piramus und Thisbe.

P. Sq. Die wollen wir euch den Augenblick hermachen.

Seren. Jhre Majestät verstehen den Titul nicht wol / könt ihr uns denselben nicht etwas erklären?

P. Sq. Das kan ich besser als der Cantzler.[64]

Theodor. Bey Gott P. Sq. düncket sich keine Sau zu seyn.[65]

P. Sq. Ein schön Spiel / schön wegen der Materie, schön wegen der
Comœdianten und schön wegen der Zuhörer / lustig und trau=
rig /[66] lustig ists weil es von Liebes=Sachen handelt / trourig
weil zwey Mörde drinnen geschehen / kurtz und lang / kurtz wird
es euch seyn / die ihr zusehet / uns aber lang / weil wir es
außwendig lernen müssen. Schrecklich und erfreulich / schrecklich
weil ein grosser Löwe / so groß als ein Affe drinnen ist / dahero
es auch wol Affentheurlich[67] heissen mag. Erfreulich / weil wir
von Jhr Gestr.[68] eine gute Verehrung gewertig sind / hat hinten
und forn nichts / ihr sehet wie die Comœdi gebunden ist / sie hat
vornen nichts und hinten auch nichts.[69] Niemals vor tragiret und
noch nie gedrucket. Jch bin erst vor 3. Tagen mit fertig worden /
derowegen ist nicht glaublich / daß sie zuvor tragiret oder gedruckt
sey.

Theodor. Sie wird ja aber in künfftig gedrucket werden.

P. Sq. Ja freylich / und ich wil sie Jhrer Majestät dediciren, durch
P. Sq. der bin ich / Schulmeister daselbst / das ist zu Rumpels=
Kirchen.

Cassandra. Wer wolte das errathen?

P. Sq. Wer es nicht kan / dem steht es frey / daß er es bleiben lasse.
Jch richte mich nach dem Cantzley Stylo. Neulich bekam ich einen
Brieff / der war unterschrieben datum Kunrathsheim durch Peter
Aschern / Stadtschreibern daselbst. Bin ich nicht so gut als er?

Seren. Jhr habt euch sehr wol verantwortet/[70] Herr Marschalck man
lasse sie in dessen tractiren. Nach vollendeter Abendmalzeit
stellet euch mit euren Gehülffen auffs fertigste[71] ein.

P. Sq. Ja / ja Juncker König / Ja.

Serenus. Bey Gott Herr Marschalck / ihr habet statliche Kurtzweil
angerichtet / wo die Tragœdi so anmuttig / wie sich der Anfang
anlässet / wird unter den Zusehern niemand eines Schnuptuches
zu Abtrucknung der Thränen bedürffen.[72]

Cassandra. Es wäre denn daß sie im Lachen hervor dringen.

Eubul. Jhre Majestät werden Wunder sehen und hören / ich hätte
selbst nimmermehr vermeinet / daß so vortreffliche Geschickligkeit
in Herren Peter Squentz vergraben.

Der Dritte Auffzug.

Die Perſonen alle.

Theodorus. Vnſere Comœdianten verziehen ziemlich lange.

Caſſandra. Gut Ding wil Zeit haben.[73]

Serenus. Ich zweiffele / daß bey ihnen das erſte / derowegen hal=
ten ſie ſich an das letzte / vielleicht wird aus der Tragœdi von
Piramo und Thisbe der Carolus quinque oder Julius unus.[74]

Violandra. Herr P. Sq. ſchiene ſonſt ziemlich leichte: Wo ihm die
andern nicht Gegenwage halten / dürffte ihn der Weſtwind ſo
weit hinwegführen / daß er von Ritter Arto nicht leicht zu ereylen.[75]

Eubul. Mich bedaucht ſie kommen. Ich höre ein gepolter vor der
Thür.

Seren. Es iſt nicht anders / Herr Peter Sq. beginnet ſich zu reuſch=
pern.[76]

Violand. Die Morgenröte bricht an / die Sonne wird bald auff=
gehen.[77]

Theodor. Man ſchaue und wundere ſich. Wenn man des Wolffes
gedencket ſo kömt er. Was wil der alte Lappe mit dem höltzernen
Ober=Rocken?[78]

Eubul. Den träget er an ſtat des Zepters / weil er ſich zum Vorreder
des Traur=Spiels auffgeworffen.

Seren. Es iſt kein Kinderwerck / wenn alte Leute zu Narren
werden.[79]

Peter Squentz beginnet nach gethaner altfränk= kiſchen Ehrerbittung ſein traurig Luſt=Spiel.[80]

P. Sq. Ich wündſche euch allen eine gute Nacht. Dieſe Spiel habe
ich Herr Peter Sq. Schulmeiſter und Schreiber zu Rumpels=
Kirchen ſelber gemacht.

Seren. Der Vers hat ſchrecklich viel Füſſe.

P. Sq. So kan er deſto beſſer gehen. Ihr[81] werden noch mehr
dergleichen folgen: nun ſtille! und macht mich nicht mehr Irre.

> Doch mangelts wol umb einen Birnenſtiel.[82]
> Fünff Actos hat das ſchöne Spiel.[83]
> Daran hab ich drey ſelber erdicht
> Die andern 2. hat M. Lollinger der Leinweber in die falten
> gericht.[84]

Ist ein Meister Sänger und kein OX,
Versteht sich wol auf Equifox,[85]
Wir haben gesessen manche liebe Nacht /
Eh' wir die frölishe Tragœdi zu wege bracht.
Nu was des Spiels Summiren summarum sey.[86]
Sag' ich euch hier mit grossem Geschrey.[87]

Hierauff verstummt er und kratzt sich im Kopff.

Cassandra. Vor diesem Geschrey kan man noch wol bleiben.

P. Sq. Nach langem stillschweigen. Je du diebischer Kopff! hast du den Dreck[88] denn gar müssen vergessen! Nun das ist die erste Sau / der Comœdianten sind 7. Wenn ein jedweder eine macht / so haben wir ein halb Tutzend weniger zwo.[89] Ey hertzer lieber Herr König / habet mir doch nichts für übel / ich habe es zu Hause schlappermentsch[90] wol gekönnt / ich wils mit meinem Weibe und allen Mitgesellen bezeugen. Ey. Ey. Ey. Ey.

Er suchet eine lange weile den Zettel / als er ihn zu letzt in dem lincken Ermel funden / da setzt er die Prülle auff / und sihet auffs Papier / darnach fähret er fort.

Ein kühner Degen heist Piramus.
Der Tragiret den ersten Actus.
Die Liebe / der reubichte[91] schäbichte Hund /
Hat ihm seine 5. Sinnen verwundt /
Er klaget über die liebliche Pein /
Vnd wolte so gerne erlöset seyn.
Die Thisbe find sich bey der Wand /
Vnd redet durch das Loch mit Verstand.

Serenus. Hilff Gott das sind treffliche Vers.

Cassandra. Nach Art der alten Pritschmeister Reymen.[92]

Theodorus. Wenn sie besser wären / würden wir so sehr nicht drüber lachen.[93]

P. Sq. Thisbe zeucht aus in schneller Eyl
Dem Piramus seinen Liebes=Pfeil /
Vnd klaget ihm daß ihr die Lieb
Gekruchen in den Bauch so trieb.[94]
Als sie geschlaffen unter dem Baume faul /
Vnd auffgelassen ihr grosses Maul /
Piramus verspricht ihr zu helffen /

Sagt / sie solte nicht so gelffen /[95]
Bestellet sie zu einem Brunnen /
Bey dem Mondenschein / nicht bey der Sonnen.
Als sie dahin sich nun begeben
Kommet ein grimmiger Löwe eben.
Sie erschrickt und läfft den Mantel fallen /
In dem thut Piramus auch herwallen /
Vnd weil sich der Löwe auff den Mantel gestreckt
Vnd Jungen droben außgeheckt /
Findet er den bluttigen Mantel /
Das macht ihm gar einen bösen Handel /
Er meint der Löwe habe Thisben gefressen /
Darumb wil er nicht mehr Brod essen /
Er ersticht sich und bleibet todt /
Genade ihm der liebe Gott.[96]
Thisbe läst sich dadurch betrügen /
Denn als sie ihn findet todt liegen /
Fällt sie in sein Schwerdt auch
Vnd ersticht sich in ihren Bauch.
Ihr dürfft euch aber nicht entsetzen/
Wenn Thisbe sich so wird verletzen /
Sie ersticht sich nicht / es ist nur Schimpff![97]
Wir wollen schon brauchen Glimpff.
Auch last euch gar nicht diß betrüben
Wenn der schreckliche grimmende brüllende Löw wird einher
     schieben.
Im übrigen sag ich euch diß fürwahr /[98]
Es sol nicht fehlen umb ein Haar /[99]
Wo ihr das Lachen nicht werdet lassen /
So werd ich euch schlagen auff die Taschen:[100]
Ich sag euch das / ihr Alten und Jungen
Ich werd euch schlagen auff die Zungen.
Speyet aus und räuschpert euch zuvor /
Vnd gebet uns denn ein liebreiches Ohr.
Ihr werdet hier schöne Sachen fassen /
Wenn ihr euch nur wollt lehren lassen:
Nun mangelts nur an diesem allein /
Daß ich euch weise die Comœdianten mein.[101]
Kompt heraus liebe Comœdianten,
Die liebe Zeit ist nun verhanden /
Daß wir unsere schöne Gedicht /
Mit der Zeit bringen an das Licht
Nun gehet dreymahl auff und nieder

Stellt euch an diese Seite wieder.
Nun tretet noch einmahl herumb /[102]
Meister Mondschein ey gehet nicht so krumb!
Meister Bullabutän / kommet zur hand
Vnd vertrit in dem Spiel die Wand /
Denn kommt Piramus unverdrossen
Auch Thisbe macht ihm Wunder Possen.
M. Kricks über und über ist der Mond /
Er scheint und leucht im höheren Thon.
Der Löwe aber stehet noch in jener Ecken /
Damit ihr ja nicht dürfft erschrecken /
Er wird aber zu rechter Zeit wol kommen
Eh' ihr es meint / hört ihr ihn nicht schon brummen?
Meister Lollinger wird Brunnen seyn /
Schaut nur wie fein er geht herein!
Nun tretet nur wieder an euren Ort
Vnd sprecht hernach wol aus alle Wort /
Ich habe itzt nicht mehr zu verrichten /
Als / daß ich sitze in diesem Winckel tichten /
Vnd gebe wol acht in meinem Büchelein /
Ob sie das Spiel tragiren sein.

Peter Sq. setzet sich auff einem Schemmel / nimt die Brülle setzet sie auff die Nasen / als er aber sein Exemplar ansehen wil / stösset ein Hofe=diener an den Schemmel / daß Peter Sq. über und über fällt / als er aufgestanden / spricht er wider den König.

P. Sq. Herr König / es giebet leider viel Narren auff eurem Hofe.[103]
Eubul. Gott lob! da kommt die Wand.
Cassand. Treffliche Erfindungen!
Serenus. Last uns hören / ob diese Wand auch reden werde?
M. Bullabut. Ihr Herren höret mir zu mit offnen Ohren /
　　　Ich bin von ehrlichen Leuten gezeuget.[104]
　　　Mein Groß=Vater ward gefangen und gebunden[105]
　　　Vnd wie man saget / so ist Er abgezogen /
　　　Mein Vater war der Bettler König /
　　　Er hat mir warhafftig gelassen nicht gar viel /
　　　Meiner Mutter hat es wol gelückt /[106]
　　　Daß man sie hat nach Fischen gesand.[107]
　　　Ich habe in meinen jungen Jahren

Warhafftig sehr viel und mancherley gelernet /
Meine Schwester hat eine schöne Stirn
Vnd darauff einen Flecken wie ein Apffel.
Es wolte sie schier keiner nehmen /
Ich darff mich meines Geschlechts nicht verdriessen.
Als ich nun herumb lieff wie ein Pracher /[108]
Thät man mich zu einem Blasebalcke Erfinder /
Als ich da gelernet in meiner Jugend /
Weißheit / Verstand und grosse Kunst.
Hat mich Herr P. Squentz tüchtig erkant /
Daß ich sol seyn in diesem Spiel die Maure /
Nun steh' ich hir auff diesem Plan /
Ihr dürfft nicht so ansehen mich /
Ich bin die Maur das solt ihr wissen /
Vnd solt es euch allen mit einander leid seyn.

Piramus **gehet etliche mahl stillschweigend auff und nieder / endlich fraget er P. Squentzen.**

Piram. Was sol ich mehr sagen?
P. Sq. Das ist die ander Sau.[109]
Pir. Das ist die ander Sau. Aber nein / es stehet nicht so in meinem Zedel.
P. Sq. Gleich wie.
Pir. Ja / ja / ja / ja / Gleich wie / Gleich wie /
Gleich wie die KühBlum auff dem Acker
Verwelckt / die früh gestanden wacker
So trucknet aus der Liebesschmertz
Der Menschen ihr gar junges Hertz.
O Wasser! O Wasser! ich brenn / ich brenn!
Daß ich mich selber nicht mehr kenn /
Ja Cupido, du Beerenhäuter /
Du hast verderbt einen guten Reuter /
O süsse Liebe / wie bistu so bitter /
Du sihest aus wie ein Moßkewitter[110]
Ey / Ey wie krübelt[111] mir der Leib /
Nach einem schönen jungen Weib!
Die Thisbe ist / die mich so plaget /
Nach der meine arme Seele fraget /
Ich weine Thränen aus / wie Flüsse
Wie ungeheure Wassergüsse /
Vnd kan sie doch nicht sprechen an /
Die Wandt hat mir den Possen gethan

Du lose Gotts verfluchte Wandt
Ich wolte daß du wärst verbrandt.
Du leichtfertige diebische Wandt
Warumb bist du nicht in Stücken gerandt?

Violandr. Das muß eine fromme Wandt seyn / daß sie sich gar nichts zu verantworten begehret.

M. Bullab. Ja ich habe nichts mehr auff meinen Zedel / darff auch nichts mehr sagen / ich wolt es ihm sonst auch wol unter die Nasen reiben.

Pir. Du lose ehrvergessene Wand.
Du schelmische / diebische / leichtfertige Wand.

M. Bullab. Ey Pickelhäring / das ist wider Ehr und Redligkeit / es stehet auch in dem Spiel nicht / du kanst es aus deinem Zedel nicht beweisen. Ich bin ein Zunfftmässiger Mann.[112] Mache / daß es zu erleyden ist / [113] oder ich schlage dir die Wand umb deine ungewaschene Gusche.

Piram. Du rotziger Blasebalckemacherischer Dieb! Solst du mich dutzen? weist du nicht / daß ich ein Königlicher Diener bin? Schau / das gehöret einem solchen Holuncken.[114]

Pickelhäring schläget Bullabután in den Hals / Bullabután schläget ihm hergegen die Wand umb den Kopff / sie kriegen einander bey den Haaren und zerren sich hurtig auff dem Schau- platz herumb / worüber die Wand schier gantz in Stücken gehet. Peter Squentz suchet sie zu scheiden.

P. Sq. Das müsse Gott im Himmel erbarmen! das ist die 3. Sau. Je schämet ihr euch denn nicht für dem Könige?[115] Meinet ihr / daß er eine Hundsfutte[116] ist? höret auff in aller Hencker Namen / höret auff / höret auff / sage ich. Stellet euch in die Ordnung / sehet ihr nicht / daß Thisbe herein kömpt?

Bullabután tritt mit der zerrissenen Wand wieder an seinen Ort.

Thisbe. Wo sol ich hin / wo komm ich her?
Ich sinne bey mir die länge und quer
Mein gantzes Herz im Leibe bricht /
Vertunckelt ist mein Angesicht /

6

Die Liebe hat mich gantz beseſſen
Vnd wil mir Lung und Leber freſſen /[117]
Ich weiß nicht / wie ſie mir den Bauch
Gemacht ſo pucklicht[118] und ſo rauch![119]
Ach Pyramus du edles Kraut
Wie haſt du mir mein Hertz zuhaut /[120]
Ach! Ach! könnt ich doch bey dir ſeyn
Mein hertzes liebes Schätzelein.
Ach / daß ich einmal bey dir wär!
Ja wenn die loſe Wand nicht wär.

Caſſand. Itzt wird es wieder über die arme Wand gehen.

Seren. Ich möchte die Wand nicht ſeyn in dieſem Spiel.

Thisbe. Doch ſchau / was ſeh' ich hier vor mir /
Ein Loch ſo groß als eine Thür.
Du liebe holdſelige Wand!
Gebenedeyet ſey die Hand /
Die ein ſolch Loch durch dich that drehen.
O könt ich doch nun Piramum ſehen
Doch ſchau! doch ſchau! er kommt gegangen
Mit einem Degen gleich einer Stangen /
Ich höre ſeine Sporne klingen
Die Muſic thut ſo lieblich ſingen
Ach ſeht ſein ſchönes kleines Maul /
Das grüſelt[121] wie ein Acker Gaul.

Piramus. Potz! hör' ich da nicht Thisben ſprechen?
Ich muß das Loch noch gröſſer brechen.

P. Sq. Brecht den Teuffel eure Mutter / es iſt ja vor zu ſtoſſen und
zu brochen genug.[122]

Piram. Liebſte Thisbe ſehet ihr mich nicht?

Thisbe. O ja! Du Königliches Angeſicht.

Piramus. Wie gehtseuch doch / mein tauſend Schatz?

Thisbe. Sehr wol nun hier auff dieſem Platz

Piramus. Ach aber ach! ich bin ſo kranck /

Thisbe. So legt euch nieder auff die Banck.

Piramus. Ach Thisbe helfft eh' ich verderb /
Vnd gar vor lauter Liebe ſterb!

Thisbe. Was ſchadt euch doch / wo thuts euch weh?

Piramus. Ich bin ſo heiß als Mertzen Schnee.[123]
Die Liebe macht mir wunderliche Poſſen /
Sie hat mich gar ins Herz geſchoſſen.
Ach zieht mir aus den harten Pfeil /
Sonſt ſterb ich in geſchwinder Eyl.

Thisbe. Wol! wol! tretet nur für das Loch

Vnd hebt den Hindern wacker hoch /
Das ist ein Pfeil sich[124] lieber sich.[124]

Piram. Ey! ey! ey! ey! wie schmertzt es mich!

Thisbe. Geduld! Er wird bald hausen[125] seyn.
Seyd ihr nun heil mein Zucker=Mündelein?
Sich[126] lieber Pfeil bistu zu stoltz
Vnd reuchst doch wie Cypressen Holtz.[127]

Piram. Ich fühle warlich nicht viel Schmertzen;
Ey blaset auff die Wunde sonder Schertzen.

Thisbe. Wie ist euch nun genung gethan?

Piram. Ey setzt noch einen Kuß daran.

Thisbe. Nun wol / ich hab es auch verricht.

Piram. Nun fühl ich weiter Schmertzen nicht.

Thisbe. Wer aber heilet meine Pein?

Piram. Ich / ich mein Turteltäubelein.

Thisbe. Ich habe geschlaffen mit offnem Mund
Vnd Cupido der schlimme Hund
Ist mir gekrochen in den Leib
Ach weh! mir armen jungem Weib!

Seren. Ich meinte es wäre eine Jungfrau.

P. Sq. Es ist generaliter, das ist in lata significatione geredet.[128]

Piram. Gib dich zu frieden meine Seel /
So bald der Mond aus seiner Höl'[129]
Wird mit blutgelbem Angesicht
Auffpfeiffen sein durchläuchtig Licht
So wollen wir beym Brunnen allein
Zusammen kommen und reden fein
Ich wil euch euren Schmertz vertreiben /
Ihr sollet meine Liebste bleiben.

Thisbe. Beym Brunnen hinter jenem End?

Piram. Bey Nachbar Kuntzen Hoffgewend.[130]

Thisbe. Gott geb' euch unterdessen gute Nacht.

Piram. Mein halbes Hertz im Leibe lacht.

Thisbe gehet wieder zurücke und spricht.

Ey Piramus / laßt euch nicht verdrüssen /
Daß ich euch anfänglich nicht konte grüssen.

Piram. Verzeiht mir auch hertzliebe Magd /
Daß ich euch keinen guten Tag gesagt.

Thisbe kommt noch einmal zurücke.

       Was mach ich in deſſen mit dem Pfeil?

Piram.   Steckt ihn in Schmeer in ſchneller eyl
       So geſchwillet nicht die Wunde mein.[131]

Thisbe kehret wiederumb.

       Wie lange muß er drinnen ſeyn?
       Iſts gnug ein Tag zwey oder vier?

Piram.   Drey iſt genug / das glaubet mir.

Thisbe.   Nun gutten Abend biß auff die Nacht:

Piram.   Schlafft Liebſte / biß ihr aufferwacht.

Eine Perſon ſiehet eine ziemliche weile durch das Loch nach der andern / biß ſich Piramus zum erſten verleuret.

Bullab.   Ade ich zieh' nun auch dahin.
       Gott lob daß ich beſtanden bin.[132]
       Ade / Ade zu gutter Nacht;
       Nehmt unterdeſſen eu'r in acht.
       Ich bitte den König mit ſeinen Knaben[133]
       Er wolte mir nichts für übel haben.

Serenus.   Blaſebalckmacher / hütte du dich / daß du darinnen nicht Händel mit dem Piramus anfangeſt / die Comœdianten irre macheſt / und das Spiel verderbeſt / ſonſt wird der Thurm nach dir ſchnappen.[134]

Bullab.   Ich habe nichts mehr zu ſagen / Herr Peter Squentz hat nichts mehr auff meinen Zedel gemachet.

Bulla Butän trit ab, Meiſter Kricks komt gegangen.

Caſſandra.   Behüt uns Gott / was ſol dieſes bedeuten?

P. Sq.   Tugendſame Frau Königin / dieſer iſt der Monde.

Theodor.   Iſt dieſer der Monde! und ſihet ſo finſter aus?

P. Sq.   Ja Herr / er iſt noch nicht in dem erſten Viertel.

Theodor.   So wolte ich wündſchen den Voll=Mond zu ſehen / ſage mir doch mein lieber Monde / warumb haſtu keine gröſſere Kertzen in die Laterne geſtecket?

M. Kr.   über und über. Das Spiel iſt kurtz / darumb muß das Licht auch kurtz ſeyn / denn wenn ſich Thisbe erſticht / muß das Licht ausgehen / denn das bedeutet / daß der Monde ſeinen Schein verlohren / das iſt verfinſtert worden.

Seren. Wir sind aber berichtet / der Mond könne nicht verfinstert
werden / er sey denn gantz voll.[135]

M. Kr. über und über. Das mag Herr Peter Squentz verant=
worten / denn diesem hat es also beliebet.

P. Sq. Ja ein Narr kan mehr fragen / als hundert weise Leute
antworten.

Violand. Dafern dieser Mond verfinstert wird / wird es ein er=
schrecklich Schauspiel seyn.

M. Kr. über und über. Freylich / aber haltet die Fressen zu /
und höret was ich sagen werde.

     Itzund kom ich herein gehuncken /[136]
     Ach lieben Leut ich bin nicht truncken /
     Ich bin gebohren von Constant /[137]
     Tinopel ist mein Vaterland /
     Ich fürchte es werd' mir immer gehn /
     Wie meinem Vater ist geschehn.
     Derselbe hatt böse Füsse
     Vnd bieß nicht gern harte Nüsse.
     Die Augen werden mir so tunckel
     Sie sehen aus wie zwey Carfunckel /
     Ich schmiede wacker früe und spat
     Vnd sage / Gott gib guten Rath /
     Ich schmiede und schlage tapffer zu /
     Was ich thu muß mein Knecht auch thun /
     Nun nehm ich an ein neuen Orden /
     Vnd bin der heilge Mondschein worden /
     Bey diesem Glantz sol Thisbe sich /
     Erstechen dencket nur an mich /
     So schein / so schein du lieber Mon /
     Der frische Brunn kommt einher gohn.[138]

Ich bin der lebendige Brun‑

nen/ purrr   purrr   purrr

Ich habe Waſſer gewon‑   nen/ im

Winter und im Som‑   mer/ Habt doch nur

kei‑   nen Kum‑   mer/ im

Sommer und im Win‑   ter/ ich habe Waſſer

vorn und hin‑   ter/ purre   purre

purre   re re re re.

Ich habe so gelauffen
Pur / pur / pur / pur / pur /
Es möchten all erſauffen.
Ihr könnt hier alle trincken /
Habt ihr nur gute Schincken /[140]
Ihr könnt euch alle laben
Ihr ſollet Waſſer gnug haben
Pyr / pyr / pyr / pyr / pyr / pyr.
Aus meinen Criſtallen Röhren
Per / per / per /
Könt ihr Waſſer lauffen hören
Ihr könnt Waſſer hören ſpringen
Nach meinem ſüſſen ſingen /
Wie ich ſinge nach den Noten
So fallen die Waſſer=Knoten.[141]
Per / per / per / per / per / per.
So lauff du helles Waſſer
Lyri / lyri / lyri / lyri / lyri.
Ich bin fürwar kein Praſſer.
Der Waſſermann im Himmel
Macht kein ſo groß Getümmel
Die Waſſer=Lüß[142] auff Erden
Mag nicht ſo ſchöne werden.
Lyri / lyri / lyri / lyri / lyri.

Theodor. Diesen Wassermann solten billich alle Calender=macher[143] ad vivum in ihre Wetterbücher setzen lassen.

Seren. Ihr Liebden?[144] der Herr Vater kan ihm pension anpræsentiren, vielleicht läst er sich in unsern Lustgarten verdingen.

Cassand. Was ist das vor[145] ein Thier mit der grünen Decke?

P. Sq. Das ist der grimmige Löwe.

Eub. Ey / man hätte ihm billich einen Zettel sollen anhefften / daß er zu nennen wäre gewesen.

M. Kl. Ihr lieben Leute erschrecket nicht.
    Ob ich gleich hab ein Löwen Gesicht
    Ich bin kein rechter Löw bey traun
    Ob ich gleich habe lange Klaun. (monstrat manus)
    Ich bin nur Klipperling der Schreiner /
    Ey Lieber glaubts ich bin sonst keiner
    Hier ist mein Schurtzfell und mein Hubel.[146]
               (monstrat præcinctorium)
    Macht doch nicht einen solchen Trubel.
    Ich bin doch ja ein armer Schinder
    Und habe das Hauß voll kleine Kinder /
    Die mir mit ihren Brodtaschen
    Das Geld in zwölff Leib[147] vernaschen;
    Die grosse Noth hat mich hieher getrieben /
    Es wär sonst wol unter wegen[148] blieben /
    Drumb hoff ich unser Herr König /
    Der werd itzund angreiffen sich.
    Und uns armen Comœdianten
    Dafern wir nicht bestehn mit Schanden /
    Ein kleine Verehrung geben
    Deßwegen tragir' ich den Löwen.

Theodor. Der Löwe kan bey Gott seine Nothdurfft wol melden / wir hören in dieser Comœdi, was uns unser lebenlang weder vor Gesichte noch Ohren kommen / sage Löwe hast du noch viel zu reden?

M. Kl. Nein / ich muß nur brüllen.

Thisbe. Gott lob / die süsse Nacht ist nun kommen!
    O hätt' ich doch nun meinen Piramus vernommen /
    Wo find ich ihn? wo ist er hin?
    Nach ihm steht all mein Hertz und Sinn.
    Ey Piramus mein Auffenthalt /[149]
    Ey bleib nicht lange! kom nur bald /
    Bey diesem Brunnen wird er erscheinen /
    Noch eher als man sol vermeinen /
    Ich wil mich hier was niedersetzen

Vnd mich mit stiller Ruh ergetzen.
Hilff Gott / was seh ich hier vor mir
Ein grimmer Löw ein böses Thier!

Der Löwe fänget an zu mauen wie eine Katze.

Thisbe. Hier bleib ich nicht es ist Zeit lauffen!
O Himmel / ich fall über den hauffen
O lieber Löwe / laß mich leben!
Ich wil dir gerne meine Schaube geben.

Sie wil die Schaube wegwerffen / kan aber nicht / weil sie zu feste angebunden / als sie endlich die Bänder zurissen /[150] schlägt sie den Löwen umb den Kopff / und laufft davon schreyend.

O weh / O weh! wie bang ist mir /
O hätt ich nur ein Tründlein Bier
Mein mattes Hertz damit zu laben /
Mir ist als wer ich schon begraben.

Thisbe **entlaufft / der Löwe stehet auff / nimt die grüne Decke gleich einem Mantel umb die Achsel / und die Schaube in die Hand und tritt neben den Monden.**

M. Kricks. Löwe du möchtest nun wol hinein gehen. Weist du nicht das Herr Peter Squentz gesaget / es stehe seltzam und Bären=häuterisch / wenn die Comœdianten auff der Bühne stehen / selber zu sehen / und Affen feyl haben wollen![151]

M. Klipperl. Nein schau! was ist dir daran gelegen. Dir zu trotz wil ich hier stehen.

M. Kr. über und über. Du hast ein Maul / man möchte es mit Säudreck füllen / und mit Eselsfürtzen[152] verbrämen. Gehe vor den Hencker hinein / oder ich wil dir Beine machen.

Mester Klipperl. Du lahmer Frantzösischer[153] Schmied! Du wilst mir Beine machen / ich sehe der Comœdi so gerne zu als du oder ein anderer / trotz dir gesaget!

M. Loll. Haltet / haltet stille! ihr werdet mich umbstossen / und mir das Wasser gar verschütten!

M. Kricks. Was ist daran gelegen?

Der Mond schlägt dem Löwen die Laterne umb den Kopff / der Löwe erwischet den Monden bey den Haaren / in diesem Getümmel werffen sie den Brunnen umb / und zerbrechen ihm den Krug / der Brunn schläget beyden die Schärben umb die Ohren / P. Sq. wil Fride machen / wird aber von allen dreyen darnieder gerissen / und bekommt sein theil Schläge auch darvon.

M.   Loll.   Ey es ist schade umb meinen schönen Topff / er kostet mich 8. weisse Groschen und 3. Hel.

P.   Sq.   Friede / Friede / Pax vobis! schämet ihr euch nicht! haltet inn / haltet inn / Meister Mondenschein lasset gehen / Meister Brunn stehet auff. Haltet inn / sage ich / wer nicht auffhöret / sol keinen Heller bekommen. Schämet euch doch vor ehrlichen Leuten. Meister Löwe von hir! von hir. Meister Mondenschein tretet wieder in die Ordnung / Thisbe holet einen andern Krug heraus. Meister Mondenschein lauffet geschwinde / und zündet das Liecht wieder an / das war eine erschreckliche Sau!

Seren.   Der Mond hat den Löwen ziemlich beleuchtet /[154] ich halte er werde morgen braun und blau außsehen.

Eubul.   Der Monde ist in dem Zeichen des Löwen[155] gewesen / und wird vielleicht auch nicht leer außgegangen seyn.

Violand.   Es ist eine erschreckliche Monden Finsternüß in dem Löwen gewesen. Wir möchten wissen was sie bedeuten würde.

P.   Sq.   Was sol sie bedeuten? den Teuffel den elenden! und gutte Schläge.

Theod.   Wir stunden in Meynung / der Löwe würde auff der Thisben Mantel junge Löwen gebären / wird dieses nicht auch zusehen seyn.

P.   Sq.   Meister Klipperling vermeinte / er hätte keine junge Löwen in dem Leibe / derowegen könte er auch keine außhecken.

Theod.   Wie ists Herr Squentz. Wo bleiben die Personen? Wird niemand mehr hervor kommen?

P.   Sq.   Ho Piramus! Piramus Piramus ho! machet doch fort / wir müssen den König nicht warten lassen wie einen Narren.

Thisbe.   Piramus ist nicht hier. Er ist hinunter gegangen / und hat nur einmal trincken wollen. Darzu rieß es ihn so sehr im Leibe.

P.   Sq.   Das wird wieder eine rechte Sau werden. Ey hertzer lieber Herr König / habt mirs doch nicht vor übel / ihr sehet ja / daß es meine Schuld nicht sey / herein Piramus, daß euch der Geyer wieder hinaus führe.[156]

Piram. Diß ist die fröliche Stund /
　　　　Darvon ich Thisbe deinen Mund
　　　　Recht küssen sol hinten und vorn /
　　　　Ich mein' sie sitzt bey jenem Born!
　　　　Wie werd ich dich mein Schatz umbfangen
　　　　Nach dem mich lange thät verlangen /
　　　　Ist sie nicht hir bey diesem Born
　　　　Was hab' ich mich so viel verworn!
　　　　Eh diese Stund ankommen ist /
　　　　Nun wil ich kürtzlich sonder List
　　　　Sie fassen in den zarten Arm
　　　　Vnd drücken / daß ihr Hertz wird warm.
　　　　Wie ist daß nicht ihr Mantel hier /
　　　　Was gilts sie ist noch gar alhier?
　　　　O lieber Gott was sol das seyn!
　　　　Der Mantel blutet wie ein Schwein /
　　　　Daß man itzt abgestochen hat
　　　　Helfft lieben Freunde / was nun Rath?
　　　　Ein grimmes Thier hat sie erbissen /
　　　　Mir ist als hätt' ich in die Hosen gesch.[157]
　　　　Du grimmiges / böses wildes Thier
　　　　Hättest du nur Dreck gefressen dafür /
　　　　So wer dirs Maul nicht fedrig worden[158]
　　　　Ey! Ey! das ist ein böser Orden /
　　　　Ey was werd ich nun erdencken!
　　　　Ich werde mich für Angst erhencken /
　　　　Ey nein / der Strick ist viel zu teur /
　　　　Der Hanff ist nicht gerahten heur /[159]
　　　　O hätt ich meinen Degen bey mir
　　　　Mein Bauch den wolt ich geben dir /
　　　　Die Liebe hat mich so besessen /
　　　　Daß ich mein Schwerdt daheim vergessen.
　　　　Ich mag doch länger nicht hie bleiben /
　　　　Ich werde mich gewiß entleiben /
　　　　Ich lauffe mit dem Kopffe wider die Wand
　　　　Oder ersteche mich mit der Hand.

Er laufft und fällt über seinen Degen.

　　　　Nein lieber sich[160] was sol das seyn /
　　　　Hab ich doch hier das Schwerdte mein.
　　　　Allons! nun ists mit mir gethan
　　　　Mein lieber Hals du must daran.

> Ey es ist warlich schad umb mich /
> Frisch auff mein Hertz und dich erstich.[161]

Er zeucht den Degen aus / wendet sich gegen den Zusehern und spricht.

Erschrecket nicht lieben Leute / ich ersteche mich nicht recht / es ist nur Spiel / wer es nicht sehen kan / der gehe hinaus oder mache die Augen zu / biß ich die schreckliche That verrichtet habe.

> Nun gesegne dich Gott trincken und essen /
> Ihr Byrnen und ihr Aepffel / ich muß euer vergessen;
> Ade Ade all alt und jung /
> Der Todt thut nach mir einen Sprung.
> Gesegne euch Gott klein und groß
> Der Todt gibt mir itzt einen Stoß.

Er ziehlet eine lange weile mit dem Degen / hernach wendet er sich zu den Zuhörern und spricht.

Ey Lieber[162] fürchtet doch euch nicht so / es hat nichts zu bedeuten / Seht / ich wil mich nur mit dem Knopffe erstechen.

Hernach macht er das Wambst auff / setzet den Knopff an die Brust / die Spitze an die Bühne / fällt nieder / stehet hernach wieder auff / laufft umb das gantze Theatrum herumb und fanget an.

> Nun hab ich mich gethan vom Brod /
> Seht Lieber seht / ich bin stein tod /
> Ach wie wird Thisbe mich beklagen /
> Ey Lieber / lassts ihr doch nicht sagen.
> Ade mein Leben hat ein End
> Hie fall ich auff Bauch / Kopff und Händ.

Er fället wieder nieder / heulet eine lange weile / verkehret die Augen im Kopffe / und schweiget endlich / der Monden lescht sein Licht aus.

Theodor. Das ist ein erschrecklicher Tod / wer ihn nur recht be=
　　weinen könte.
Thisbe. Sage Mond / wo ist dein güldner Schein hinkommen /
　　Wie hast du so sehr abgenommen?
　　Vorhin warest du lieblich und klar /
　　Itzt bist du finster gantz und gar.
　　Wo werd ich den Piramus finden?
　　Ich seh ihn noch nicht dort dahinden /
　　Ich habe mich so müde gelauffen /
　　Mich dürst so; möcht ich nur eins sauffen.
　　Ich wil ihn suchen in dem Graß
　　Dort bey dem Brunn; was ist das?

Sie fället über Piramum, steht auff und besihet ihn.

　　Hilff Gott! es ist mein Piramus,
　　Ich wil ihm stehlen einen Kuß /
　　Dieweil er schläfft in dieser Ecken
　　Vnd sich ins grüne Graß thut strecken /
　　So kan ich sagen unverholen /
　　Daß ich ihm einen Schmätzerling abgestohlen.

Sie küsset ihn / Piramus schnappet nach ihr mit dem Maul.

Thisbe. Schaut Lieber wie ist er so kalt /
　　Vnd hat so eine bleiche Gestalt;
　　Schaut wie ihm hangt der Hals und Kopff
　　Ach er ist todt der arme Tropff!
　　Ey Lieber / er hat sich erstochen
　　Fürwar ich hab es wol gerochen.
　　Ach / ach / ach / ach / was fang ich an!
　　Ach Thisbe was hast du gethan?
　　Die Haar wil ich ausrauffen mir.

Sie greifft unter die Armen.　　　　　　(ridet)

　　Vnd dich beweinen für und für /
　　O Piramus du edler Ritter /
　　Du allerschönster Muscowitter /[163]
　　Ey Piramus bist du denn todt?
　　Ey sage mir doch für der letzten Noth /
　　Nur noch ein einiges[164] Wörtlein
Piram. Ich habe nichts mehr in meinem Zedelein.[165]

Violand. Das gehet noch wol hin / wenn die Todten reden können.

P. Sq. Beym S. Stentzel /[166] Piramus ihr seyd ja todt / schämet euch für dem Teuffel! ihr müßt nichts sagen / sondern stille liegen wie eine todte Sau.

Piram. Ja / ja / ja ich wils schon machen!

Thisbe. Was mach ich denn nu auff der Welt?

> Ich achte nun kein Gutt und Geld
> Ich werde mich wol auch erstechen
> Oder mir ja den Hals entzwey brechen.
> O hätt ich nur den Pfeil allhie /
> Ich stäche mir den in die Knie /
> Doch er ist weit daheim im Schmeer[167]
> Schaut / hier liegt Piramus Gewehr.
> Gutte Nacht liebes Mütterlein /
> Es muß einmal gestorben seyn;
> Gute Nacht lieber alter Vater /
> Ihr allerschönster grauer Kater.
> Mein Piramus ich folge dir
> Wir bleiben beysammen für und für /
> Ade mein liebes Mäuselein /
> Ich steche mich in mein Hertzhäuselein.

Sie sticht sich mit dem Degen unter den Rock / wirfft hernach den Degen weg / und fällt auff Piramum, spricht

> Schaut alle / nun bin ich verschieden
> Vnd lieg' allhier und schlaff' im Frieden.

Piram. Ey Thisbe, es schickt sich nicht also / die Weiber müssen unten liegen.

Cassand. Erbärmlicher Zufall / ich habe gelacht / daß mir die Augen übergehen.

Violand. Wer wird denn die Todten begraben?

Piram. Wenn die Comœdianten abgegangen sind / wil ich Thisben selber weg tragen.

Der Mond und Brunnen gehen stille davon / Piramus stehet auff / Thisbe springet ihm auff die Achseln / Piramus trägt sie mit hinweg.

P. Sq. Vorhin war ich ein Prologus[168]

> Itzund bin ich der Epilogus
> Hiermit endt sich die schöne Comœdie,

Oder wie mans heißt die Tragœdie,
Darauß ihr alle solt nehmen an
Lehr / Trost und Warnung jederman
Lernet hieraus / wie gut es sey
Daß man von Liebe bleibe frey.
Lernet auch / wenn ihr habt eine Wund
So zijt den Pfeil hinauß zur stund /
Vnd stecket ihn in eine Pechmeste /
So heilt es bald / ihr lieben Gäste
Das ist fürwar ein schöne Lehr.
Ey lieber sagt / was wolt ihr mehr?
Doch tröstet euch daß es sey schön /
Wenn man die Todten sijt auffstehn /
Ihr Jungfrauen nehmet diß in acht /
Vnd diese Warnung wol betracht:
Daß wenn ihr im Graß schlaffen wollt /
Ihr nicht den Mund auffmachen sollt /
So kreucht die Lieb' euch nicht in Hals
Die Liebe die verderbet all's
Weiter sol sich auch niemands wundern /
Das Wand / Löw / und auch Brunn besondern /
In diesem Spiel haben geredt
Mit wolbedacht man dieses thät /
Der Kirchen=Lehrer Æsopus[169] spricht
Daß ein Topff zu dem Topff sich gericht
Vnd ihm Gesellschafft angetragen
Aber der eine wolts nicht wagen /
Auch narriret[170] der Löw den Schafen
Vnd thut sie umb Muthwillen straffen;
Derhalben kan es gar wol seyn /
Daß hier redet / Löw und Brunnen fein.
Daß wir es so getichtet haben /
Daß ein Todter den andern begraben /
Dasselbe ist geschehen mit Fleiß /
Mercket hievon was ich weiß /[171]
Ein Christe trug einen todten Juden /
Den sie ihm auff die Schulter luden /
Vnd als er nun ging seinen Weg
Kam er zu einem engen Steg /
Beim selben stund ein tieffer Brunn /
Der Christ war heiß vom Jud und Sonn /
Drumb wolt er trincken frisches Wasser /
Aber der Jude / der lose Prasser /

Vberwug und zog so fein /
Den Christen mit inn Brunnen nein /
So hat der todte Jude begraben /
Den lebendigen Christen=Knaben /
Drumb glaubt / daß man es wol erlebt /
Daß ein Todter den andern begräbt /
Es sey Winter / Sommer oder Lentz /

Wündscht euch zu guter Nacht der Schulmeister und Kirchschreiber zu Rumpels=Kirchen Herr Peter Squentz.

Telos, Amen, dixi, finis, Ende.[172]

Theodor. So hat nun diese Tragœdie ein Ende.

P. Sq. Ja Woledelgeborner Herr König / und mangelt nichts mehr als das Tranckgeld.

Theodor. Wie / wenn wir es mit demselbten Actu machten / wie ihr mit der Geburt der jungen Löwen? das ist / denselbten gar außliessen.

P. Sq. Ey das müste der Teuffel haben! Ey Herr König / was Narret ihr euch viel? Ich weiß wol ihr könnets nicht lassen / ihr werdet uns ja was geben müssen?

Theodor. Herr Squentz / wir sehen daß euch bißweilen Witz gebricht.

P. Sq. Vester Juncker König / Geld auch.

Theodor. Nun wir wollen sehen / wie der Sachen zu rathen. Lasset uns hören / wie viel Säu ihr gemacht in eurer Tragœdie.

P. Sq. Herr König / ich weiß nicht wie viel ihr gezehlet habet: Ich kam mit der Rechnung biß auff zehen.

Theodorus. Was kostet eine Sau[173] so groß als ihr in eurem Dorffe?

P. Sq. Eine Sau? Eine Sau so groß als ich? die kostet / laß schauen / wie viel giebet man vor eine Sau? zwölffe auch 15. gute Gülden.

Theodor. Nun saget mir: zehnmahl 15. wie viel macht das Gülden?

P. Sq. Bald / bald / verziehet / ich wil es in die Regul detri[174] setzen / eine Sau umb 15. Gülden / wie hoch kommen zehen Säue?

Er schreibet mit Kreide auff die Bühne / hernach fanget er an /

Auff den Füssen kommen sie.

Seren. Es fehlet nicht umb ein Haar /[175] lehret ihr denn eure Schüler nicht rechnen?

P. Sq. Ja freylich! Wolweiser Juncker / vor wen sehet ihr mich an?
Seren. Was haltet ihr denn vor eine Weise?
P. Sq. Wenn sie können 1. mal 1. ist eins / und 2. mal 2. ist sieben /
so gebe ich ihnen außgelernet / und mache sie zu Rechenmeistern /
so gut als Seckerwitz und Adam Riese.[176]
Seren. Diß müssen vortreffliche Leute werden.
P. Sq. So schlimm als kein Rentmeister.
Theodor. Wol wol! Marschalck man befehle dem Schatzmeister /
daß man den Comœdianten so vielmal 15. Gülden gebe / als sie
Säue gemacht.
P. Sq. Grossen danck / grossen danck lieber Herr König / hätten wir
dieses gewüst / wir wolten mehr Säu gemachet haben. Doch ich
höre wol / wir bekommen nur Tranckgeld für die Säu / und für
die Comœdi nichts. Aber es schadet nicht. Wir sind hiermit wol
vergnüget. Gute Nacht Herr König. Gute Nacht Frau Königin:
gute Nacht Juncker / gute Nacht Jungfer / gute Nacht ihr Herren
alle mit einander / nehmet vor dieses mahl mit unsern Säuen
vor gut / auff ein andermahl wollen wir derer mehr machen /
und so grosse / als der grösseste Bauer / der unter dem gantzen
Hauffen gewesen.
Theodor. Kurtzweils gnug vor diesen Abend / wir sind müder vom
Lachen / als vom Zusehen. Daß man die Fackeln anzünde / und
uns in das Zimmer begleite.

E N D E .

7

COMMENTARY

The student who has little experience of seventeenth-century German texts will find it helpful to read the first part of the *Commentary* to the present editor's edition of *Carolus Stuardus*.

1. The first pointer to Squentz's character.
2. Cp. pp. xli–xliii.
3. A reference to the function of this farce as light relief to the performance of one of his tragedies, probably *Cardenio und Celinde*.
4. The inference we make is that the play was one of Gryph's earliest and remained in manuscript for a number of years. Cp. pp. lv–lvi.

5. The atmosphere of knockabout comedy is suggested here. Squentz comes from Rumpelskirchen, i.e. a crazy, tumble-down town.
   Meifter Krix (Krids), über unb über. The name is probably intended to convey the 'clink' of the smith's hammer on the anvil: „über unb über" no doubt refers to the overarm swinging movement. Cp. p. lii.
   Bulla Butäin. A corruption of Shakespeare's Bully Bottom. Cp. pp. xlii–xliii.
   Klipperling means a mallet used by a joiner or carpenter.
   Lollinger. Cp. p. xlvii.
   Klotz=George. Cp. p. lii.
   Zufehenbe Perfonen. The palace of Theseus in Shakespeare's play has given way to the residence of a German prince. He, his family, and his court constitute the audience of the play within the play.
   In the first edition of the play „Eubulus" appears as „Eububus" in the *dramatis personae* and in the play. The second edition has „Eubulus" in the *dramatis personae* and „Eububus" in the text. Braune (*op. cit.*, p. v) is probably right in his theory that in the second edition the author corrected the name but only in the *dramatis personae*. It is interesting to recall that in Samuel Israel's play about Pyramis and Thisbe (*c.* 1601), one of the *Ratsherren* is named Eubulus. In the present edition „Eubulus" is retained throughout.

6. Note the contrast between the pompous and extensive mode of address, and the simple, laconic answer.
7. Tuchhafft—a pun on „Tuch" and „Tugenb."
8. Verfchraubet euch, etc. The style is reminiscent of the affected speech in seventeenth-century France, lampooned in Molière's *Précieuses Ridicules* (1659). Gryphius had spent over a year in Paris and neighbourhood between 1644 and 1645.
9. Squentz speaks of *seven* senses—perhaps a development to extreme absurdity

38

of the hyperbole in the mode of address he uses to the mechanicals; or perhaps just one of several instances of ignorance displayed by Squentz.

10. Anſchlägigen Kopff—note the pun.

11. Neu=Zembla—Novaya Zemlya (New Land), a group of two islands off the north coast of Russia in the Arctic Circle, was first reached in 1594 by the Dutch navigator Willem Barents, who returned there two years later. One of his companions Gerrit de Veer published a description of the expedition in Amsterdam (1598). An English translation was edited for the Hakluyt Society (2nd ed. 1876). Gryphius will no doubt have read the original version whilst in Holland.

12. Note the verbal somersault—a comic device with a deeper import which occurs at intervals in this play.

13. Phaebussin—probably, as Palm assumed, a misprint for Phoebussin. This would be one of several instances of Squentz's pseudo-scholarship. This name is presumably a feminine form of Phoebus, an epithet of Apollo. One of the powers ascribed to Apollo was that of prophecy (cp. the oracle of Delphi). Here then, Squentz has created a new goddess who can prophesy; a "Mrs Phoebus" as it were. The suffix—in, as in "Gottschedin," gives the name a decidedly 'bourgeois' flavour—hardly suitable for a goddess! Fama was a goddess in Roman mythology, but daughter of Terra. Fama also means "rumour." The 1698 edition has "Phoebussin." Cp. *Horrib.*, II, 7.

14. Note the paradoxical use of attributives, and compare Squentz's speech at the end of Act II with *A Midsummer Night's Dream*, Act I, Sc. 2: "*Quince:* Marry, our play is The most lamentable comedy, and most cruel death of Pyramus and Thisby." This is reminiscent of Thomas Preston's *Cambises* which, the title page tells us, is "a lamentable tragedie mixed full of plesant mirth." Preston was one of the 'rhyming mother wits' who were the butt of Shakespeare's satire in the *Dream* and elsewhere. Later in this first scene of *Peter Squentz*, Pickelhäring insists on a strict separation of laughing matter from sad occasions. The seventeenth-century grammarians would not hear of a mingling of tragedy with comedy.

15. Another instance of the verbal somersault.

16. A colossal blunder which goes unnoticed by the illiterate mechanicals. Ovid was in fact looked upon with disfavour by the Church as a pagan author of doubtful moral value. The work which Squentz has in mind is the *Metamorphoses*, a collection of legends and fables covering the period from the Creation to the time of Julius Caesar. The story of Piramus and Thisbe appears in the fourth book. The rendezvous there mentioned is a fountain at the tomb of Ninus, reputed founder of the city of Ninus or Nineveh. The engraving depicting the tragedy of Thisbe in Boccaccio's *De Claris Mulieribus* (Ulm: Zainer, 1473) shows a fountain on Ninus' tomb. It is reproduced in Madeleine Doran's *Endeavors of Art*, p. 374.

17. ihm zu Trotz = like him.

18. This is probably a reference to the extemporisation on which the clown relied when playing his part. But cp. *A.M.N.D.*, Act I, Sc. 2: "*Snug.* Have you the lion's part written? pray you, if it be, give it me, for I am slow of study. *Quince.* You may do it extempore, for it is nothing but roaring." Gottsched was later to ban the technique of playing extempore.

19. Possibly not so much a courtesy extended to this particular clown (although he is a court jester) as a general recognition of the considerable status of the Fool in play production.

20. Note the play on words.

21. tapffer = wa<ter.
22. The prologue to serious drama was given a dignity it could hardly maintain in farcical comedy. In Shakespeare's time there was a widespread tradition, possibly originating in Italy, that the prologue to a tragedy should be spoken by a garlanded figure in a long cloak. (Cp. Creizenach: *Geschichte des neueren Dramas*, Vol. II, p. 295, Vol. IV, p. 313.)
23. It is characteristic of the difference in tone of the German version and that of Shakespeare's episode, that the English play mentions only the nervousness of women in general, and not of pregnant women.
24. Members of the guilds were expected to observe a certain code of conduct; e.g. to deprive a living thing of life would probably entail expulsion.
25. Früß = Fries.
26. Whether or not we are prepared to concede Klotz-George the wit, Gryphius doubtless intended a play on words here; i.e. „geſcheiden" could be a hybrid form of „geſcheid" and „beſcheiden."
27. Cp. note 16.
28. The pun should not be overlooked; „ſchwer" is to be understood literally as well as figuratively. We notice Pickelhäring is speaking.
29. In the seventeenth century the calendar was a repository for astrological and cosmological lore, horoscopes, weather forecasts, and so on (cp. Kepler's horoscope of Wallenstein). The preparation of such calendars called for considerable draughtmanship; they were not mass-produced and consequently were often regarded as valuable heirlooms.
30. Puſch = Buſch, i.e. a bundle or pencil of rays.
31. Corruption of „Valentin."
32. Picke = mod. German "Pike," not "Picke."
33. Mixture or plaster of loam and perhaps straw.
34. What Squentz means to say is *nihil ad rem*.
35. A frame.
36. The phrase seems to echo the reputation the Swabians had of yore for unpleasant personal habits, and in particular the wiping of mucus from the nose on the sleeve. The slimy herring-snout would blend exactly with a sleeve soiled in this way. Cp. the saying „Es paßt wie Rotz auf den Ärmel" (Wander: *Deutsches Sprichwörterlexicon*, Bd. 3, Sp. 1191). Cp. also Grimm: *Wörterbuch*, IV, Tl. 2, Sp. 1107; Aurbacher: *Die Abenteuer der sieben Schwaben*; Keller: *Die Schwaben in der Geschichte des Volkshumors*, p. 347; Seiler: *Deutsche Sprichwörterkunde*, p. 301. The following couplet occurs in the second chapter of Scheidt's translation of Dedekind's *Grobianus*, II, 241 et seq. (ed. Milchsack, *Neudrucke*, Nos. 34–35):

Auf beide ermel wüſch den rotz
Daß wer es ſeh vor unluſt kotz

37. Since the medieval religious plays the misunderstanding of foreign (generally Latin) words had been a source of comedy on the European stage.
38. The simile is all the more piquant because of the association of the Fool's name with pickled herring (Pökelhering).
39. Perhaps Squentz's rejoinder is rather flippant, but at all events it prompts Pickelhäring to let drop an interesting remark about the type of clown known as Jean Potage on the contemporary stage. Despite his French name, and Palm's pronouncement that he was "der Hanswurst der französischen Posse," this figure seems not to have been known as such in the French theatre. That in Germany he had a distinct personality, peculiar dress, and

mannerisms is vouched for by a seventeenth-century political pamphlet described in detail by A. C. Loffelt in the *Shakespeare-Jahrbuch*, Vol. IV, p. 378. (Cp. illustration facing p. liv above.)

"Gesprech
zwischen dem
Englischen Bickelhering
und
Frantzösischen Schanpetasen
über das
Schändliche Hinrichten
Königl. Majestät in Engeland
Schott- und Irrland.
(without place or date. 16 pages 4⁰.)

The title-page is adorned with a very interesting engraving, representing Schampetasche (*sic*) — no doubt a corruption of the typical hero of the old French farces, Jean Potage — and Bickel-Hering (Pickleherring), the English comic type. The two figures, of about a finger's length, are remarkable as giving, most probably, a faithful representation of the stage costume of the two popular heroes at that period (about 1649). Each figure is marked with its name.

Schampetasche is accosted as a Frenchman by the other speaker:

„. . . . du kanst auch nur auff gut Calvinisch unserm Herrn Gott die Schuld geben, wie kanstu doch so leichtfertig von einer solchen Schandthat reden, ich glaub ihr Frantzmänner, wenn ihr hättet gekunt und ihr euren König in euren Klauen gehabt, ihr hättet ihm eben dürffen so mitspielen, und hernach, wie unsere erbare Vögel, auch die Regierung an sich ziehen.

Schanpetase.

Wer weisz, ob es nicht besser wäre, durch viele geregieret zu werden, als von einem.

Bickelhering.

Halts Maul, du Affengesicht,¹) du verstehest die Sache nicht, etc."

¹) Among the common people in England monkey is still a favourite nickname for a Frenchman.

Jean Potage is dressed in a short, loose jacket, long and very wide trousers and a small mantle hanging from one shoulder; he wears a broad-brimmed, flappy hat, and has the traditional wooden sword in his hand. Pickleherring, who calls himself an Englishman, is dressed military-like; his figure reminds us of Shakespeare's swaggering Pistol and Ben Jonson's Captain Bobadill. His hat is like a Tyrolian hat, but twice as high, and decorated with two very long cock's feathers; he wears a short, closely-fitting jacket with big buttons, an excessively broad ruff, short but wide trousers and low shoes; a short sword or cutlass completes his costume. The last lines of the „Gesprech" have an allusion to their dress:

„Schanpetase.

Unser Herr Gott ist ein gerechter Gott, wird es wohl enden und wenden, dasz die Unschuldigen erhalten, hingegen die schuldigen ihren wohlver-dienten Lohn, wie dem Blutsrath adhaerenten, dem Dorislaw im Haag schon widerfahren, empfangen werden.

Bickelhering.

Nun so mag es seyn, ich gedenke mir auch noch ein neu Mänteligen davon zu tragen.

Schanpetase.

Und ich eine neue und bessere Schlappe, die ich ein halb Schock mal uff alamodische Art verändern kann."

As to the word Pickleherring or Pickelhäring, in the histrionic sense, I think the etymologists are too deep. They say pickeln means in Low-Saxon to cut jokes, and häring the old word hringi, that is chief, principal; and so Pickelhäring: first joker, chief clown. Why can the word not simply be a nickname? There seems to have existed a mysterious relation between the favourite jester and the favourite dish of a nation. The French had their Jean Potage, the Germans their Hans Wurst, the Italians their Maccheroni—why not the English their Pickleherring? I was sometimes inclined to see in Pickleherring (Dutch: Pekelharing) a Dutchman by origin, as the Dutch are celebrated for their pekelharing, and very fond themselves of „Hollands Zee-banket" (Holland's sea-confection) as they poetically call it. However I have relinquished the hope of ever being able to call Pickleherring my countryman. Our old comedies and farces bear no traces at all of any family connexion with him, and in our later pieces the name seems to have been borrowed from the Germans.[1])

[1]) Andreas Gryphius (1616–1664) has in his Herr Peter Squentz a Pickelhäring „des Königs lustiger Rath." G's works were known and some of them imitated in Holland; Adriaan Leeuw translated in 1659 Leo Armenius „vertaald maar besnoeid naar het Duitsch van Gryphius." Isaac Vos wrote about the same time Pekelharing in de kist. I cannot say if it is an imitation or an original piece, but Isaac Vos (not Jan) was acquainted with the German language.

It may be that the Germans received their pickleherring from England, and that the common people, amused when they got not only English pickleherring, but English actors too, thought it a capital joke to apply the name of the fish also to the new importation. In Holland the popular and old nickname for an Englishman is „Engelsche bokking", English red-herring, which seems to support my conjecture. As in the eyes of the people the clown was the principal actor, the favourite term may subsequently have been conferred on him alone.

Is it not curious that in Germany the English jester was also sometimes called Jann Posset?—Posset was another favourite English dish or drink. Jacob Ayrer has written Ein Fasznacht-Spiel, von dem Engelandischen Jann Posset."

40. This word has additional 'point', because Pickelhäring is a professional "Narr"!
41. barmherßig = erbarmenswert.
42. Cp. English "chops." Jhm = sich.
43. Kricks ignores the possibility of illusion on which the success of the play should depend.
44. The sixteenth and seventeenth centuries saw the fashioning of beautiful fountains on the continent.
45. Gryphius has his tongue in his cheek!

46. The reference is firstly to the Augustusbrunnen in front of the Rathaus in Augsburg. It is surmounted by a statue of the Emperor Augustus who founded the town. Secondly to the Neptunsbrunnen in front of the Rathaus in Danzig. At the time of Gryph's residence in Danzig, many of the rich patricians had elaborate fountains in the interior of their houses. „Clinctunus" is probably Pickelhäring's own corruption of „Neptunus."

47. Pickelhäring lives up to his reputation for obscenities.

48. The nine muses.

49. As a Meistersänger Lollinger speaks with reverence of the Master, but for Gryphius himself the words are ironical. Judging from his plays known to us, Gryphius believed that the comic element should be banned from tragedy. He certainly frowned on the love story in tragedies (cp. preface to *Leo Armenius*). Cp. note 14 above.

50. It is by no mere chance that these words are allotted to the Meistersänger. Here and in the following lines Gryphius is indulging in banter against the Meistersänger and their art.

ACT II

51. Eubulus has not been deceived by Squentz's display of 'scholarship', and he knows the nature of the entertainment the mechanicals will provide.

52. It is just possible that here Gryphius is covertly voicing his disapproval of the patronage widely bestowed on casual and itinerant players by seventeenth-century German princes and of the comparative neglect suffered by the school theatres.

53. The Squentz repertoire totals, apart from *Piramus und Thisbe*, eleven plays compared with Shakespeare's three. Meyer v. Waldeck (*op. cit.*) shows that nine of these plays have the same subject matter as certain works of Hans Sachs, whilst *Susanna* was an old favourite.

54. ſchlecht = ſchlicht, but the pun is obvious.

55. A mode of address used in contemporary comedy, more often than not by the clown.

56. In Squentz's reference to „Oberland" here and later on, there was possibly laughing matter for a seventeenth-century Silesian audience. The „Ober= länder" would be the inhabitants of part of the hilly country now known as the Sudeten mountains. Breslau and Glogau were in the lowlands.

57. The portentous manner in which Squentz recites his 'attainments' must strike his audience as ludicrous. The use of „Handlanger" in this context is of course amusing. In his last words there is genuine humour.

58. This self-applauding speech is rather a piece of jesting than serious argument, and the 'logic' is reminiscent of Shakespeare's Fool. Gryphius may also be alluding here to the *Kleinstaaterei* in contemporary Germany, which had been aggravated as a result of the peace of Westphalia in 1648. Germany was split up into approximately 300 autonomous states, each of which was very jealous of its independence. The situation in Silesia was especially fantastic.

59. The king's response is politely ironical. Now follows a relentless and methodical deflation of Squentz culminating in the prince's ironical jibe

„Nun ich ſehe/ihr ſeyd ſehr wol ausgerüſtet."

60. Cp. note 31.

61. kratzt.

62. Waldeck's argument that the reference is to Sachs' *Olivier und Artus* seems reasonable. He contends that „Oſtwinb" is the sort of linguistic corruption to be expected of such illiterate folk.
63. Note the play on words. „Erſte" here is used in the sense of "greatest." „Der Andere" also means „Der Zweite."
64. The official who was the ultimate authority on titles.
65. "Peter Squentz has no low opinion of himself." The 1663 edition has „eine Sau"—obviously a misprint.
66. The question whether comic and tragic elements should be kept apart was a topical one in Gryph's day. Cp. note 14. „luſtig" is ambiguous here, meaning both jolly and erotic.
67. Affentheurlich—an allusion to Fischart's *Affentheurlich Naupengeheurliche Geschichtklitterung.* Note the pun.
68. Ihr Gestrengen = your Honour, Majesty.
69. The meaning seems to be: This play is independent and self-contained and not a mere prelude or afterpiece to a major work. If a pun on „gebunden" is intended, the reference will be to the metre.
70. Far from being bored by Squentz's nonsense, the prince is of a mind to suffer the fooling gladly.
71. promptly.
72. Bey Gott Herr Marſchalck. . . . The royal party is now prepared for the sort of buffoonery that follows.

ACT III

73. Note the ironical twist given to the proverb.
74. Serenus takes up Cassandra's words. He doubts whether the players will produce anything good, and surmises they are clinging to the latter (i.e. time); „das letzte" may also refer to the last play on their list, i.e. *Piramus und Thisbe.*
75. Violandra is being witty at the expense of one of the play titles in Squentz's repertoire: *Von Artus und dem Ostwind,* Artus being regarded here as the adversary of the Ostwind.
76. The deliberate mistaking of the banging at the door for the noise of Squentz clearing his throat in readiness for the performance is an echo of Squentz's self-aggrandisement.
77. Once again there is irony in Violandra's symbolical reference to the feast of art promised them by Squentz.
78. "What is that old fop with the wooden distaff supposed to be?" „Ober= Rocken" seems here to be equivalent to „Spinnrocken."
79. Cp. p. xv.
80. altfränckiſch = altväteriſch, altmodiſch (not pejorative).
81. Jhr = ihrer.
82. Cp. mod. German Pappenſtiel = trifle.
83. The claim that their sketch has the pseudo-classical form of five acts, is of course, not borne out when they perform it.
84. "Put together, composed" (cp. Grimm).
85. Probably, as Palm suggested, a corruption of *aequivocos,* i.e. ambiguities. The satire in these lines is Gryph's not Squentz's.
86. Another faulty Latin tag.
87. Apparently a thrust at the manner in which the prologue was declaimed in the old plays.

88. Translate by "stuff."
89. The reckoning is infantile!
90. This is yet another stage in the progressive corruption of the French oath. „Sapperment" was widely current in the Thirty Years' War, and derived from an earlier form „facferment."
91. reubidｊte = räubige, ſcḧäbidｊte = ſcḧäbige. One of the criticisms levelled at the Pritschmeister was provoked by their use of undignified language.
92. Cp. p. xlviii.
93. Cp. pp. li.
94. trieb = trüb.
95. gelſſen = ſcḧreien. The word seems to have been used as a welcome rhyme with "helfen" in Early New High German.
96. Because of the crime of suicide.
97. Joke, fun. Compare the designation of our play on the title page, viz.: „Scḧimpſſ=Spiel." Note also the constant awareness that a rôle is being played.
98. The following ten or so lines are a close imitation of the prologue in the old Shrovetide and Passion plays.
99. The meaning is: "There is no margin of doubt."
100. Taſcḧe = "ein großes, weites, klatschendes Maul" (Grimm). Cp. mod. German "Plaudertasche."
101. The name was in general use at the time, but Gryphius associates it deliberately and emphatically with this kind of illiterate and unskilled actor.
102. Apparently a contemporary custom at such dramatic performances.
103. An allusion to the institution of court jester. Cp. p. xvi.
104. Bullabutäin's speech is in rather irregular *Knittelverse*, in which Gryphius has replaced the rhyming words with a synonym, viz.:

geboren	by	geзeuget
abgeſcḧunben	„	abgeзogen
gar wenig	„	nidｊt gar viel
geſcḧicft	„	geſanb
erfaḧren	„	gelernet
Birn	„	Apſſel
ſcḧämen	„	verbrieſſen
Macḧer	„	Erſinber
Tugenb	„	Kunſt
Wanb	„	Maure
micḧ ſo ſeḧen an	„	ſo anſeḧen micḧ
verbrieſſen	„	leib ſeŋn

Gryphius is poking fun at the clumsiness of much popular verse. Cp. pp. xlviii *et seq.*
105. i.e. a serf.
106. gelücfen = glücfen = paſſieren.
107. She was drowned.
108. Pracḧer = beggar. It is a loan word of Slavonic origin.
109. Squentz is noting the blunders the company is making and when the performance is over, he receives payment for them.
110. It is possible that there is a mischievous reference here to the town of Muskau in Lower Silesia. The name occurs again on p. 33. Otherwise Muscovite was the name given to an inhabitant of Muscovy, i.e. Moscow or Russia

generally. In an applied sense it could mean strange, crude, rough. "Die Einwohner aber sind so thum, so brutal und so sclavisch, daß sie den Türcken und Tartarn nicht viel nachgeben." (*Johann Hübners, Rect. Gymn. Martisb. Kurtze Fragen aus der Alten und Neuen Geographie, zum Fundament*, etc. (1697), p. 768.) The term Muscovy glass has been in use certainly since the sixteenth century, as it was formerly used in Russia for window panes. Nowadays muscovite is used as a name for mica, of which certain varieties have a *lustre*. Perhaps this is the sense here.

111. **fribbelt.**

112. i.e. as a member of a guild, a man of honour and dignity.

113. "make it bearable," i.e. "apologise." The comedy here is that Bullabutäin, encouraged by Violandra in the audience, lays his part aside and takes Piramus' words as a personal affront. Piramus, provoked by Bullabutäin's manner, and standing on his dignity as a noble personage, adds insult to injury. The play is temporarily forgotten and the two come to blows.

114. **Holuncke** = **nackter Bettler** (Grimm); another word of Slavonic origin. Cp. mod. German „Halunke."

115. **für dem Könige** = **vor dem Könige** = in the presence of the king.

116. Older form of „Hundsfott."

117. The heart, liver, and kidneys were formerly regarded as the seat of the passions.

118. **buckelig.**

119. Probably not „rauh," but in the sense of "furred." Cp. **Rauchwerk.**

120. **zerhaut.**

121. **grüseln** = „gewisse Locktöne ausstoßen" (cp. Grimm, who says this use of the verb is obscure).

122. „Es ift ja schon zerstoßen und zerbrochen genug."

123. Snow in March can cause considerable sunburn.

124. **sich** = **sieh.**

125. **Haußen** = **hie außen** = out.

126. **sich** = **sieh.**

127. The cypress is traditionally the symbol of grief. Its tiny leaf can puncture the skin.

128. Squentz says that Thisbe's words must not be understood literally.

129. **Höhle,** i.e. hide-out, den. Note in these lines the satire on highflown, poetic style.

130. A piece of arable land belonging to the sovereign (Hof).

131. Evidently a superstitious custom.

132. Bullabutäin has got through his part and now can go off.

133. The meaning is „Knappe," i.e. courtier, attendant, squire.

134. "Or you will land in prison."

135. Note the astronomical knowledge; it is a fact that lunar eclipses always take place at full moon.

136. „hincken" was a strong verb in MHG.

137. This kind of mutilation (for the sake of rhyme) was not tolerated in the *Kunstdichtung*!

138. **gehen.**

139. Meister Lollinger's song is, of course, overt satire on the *Meistergesang*, from the pen of a scholar-poet. Note the cadences, especially the final one. Transcribed from the alto into the treble clef, the melody reads:

Ich bin der lebendi-ge Brun- nen, purrr

purrr purrr Ich habe Wasser ge-

won- nen, im Winter und im Som- mer, Habt

doch nur kei- nen Kum- mer im Sommer und im

Win- ter, ich habe Wasser vorn und hin-

ter, pur- re, pur- re, purre re re re re re.

ly- ri, ly- ri, ly- ri, ly, ri, ly- ri ly ri.

The 1663 edition has an extra semi-quaver (on g) as the penultimate note, making the final semi-breve f instead of g. This error is corrected in the present edition.

140. Schenfel, i.e. legs; presumably in the sense that those who are tall enough will be able to reach the water.
141. No doubt he is referring to the cadences.
142. Palm suggests "Wasserlisse," i.e. "Wassernixe."
143. Cp. note 29.
144. A mode of address formerly common in royal circles.
145. für.
146. Cp. note 23. Throughout the play the characters remind themselves that they are merely playing a part. Hubel = Hobel.
147. Probably a pun on „Leib" and „Laib."

148. unterwegs.
149. refuge.
150. zerriſſen.
151. Maulaffen feil haben.
152. A kind of thistle of which asses were supposed to be fond, and which made them break wind.
153. Here the adjective denotes contempt and disgust.
154. Serenus and Violandra cannot resist making puns on this farcical situation.
155. i.e. in the Zodiac. In phrenology the qualities created by the sign of Lec were pride, ambition, and domination.
156. Cp. the saying "daß dich der Geier hole!"
157. The word is similarly mutilated in the 1663 edition.
158. The meaning seems to be: if only you had eaten nothing better than rubbish previously (dafür = davor = zuvor), your appetite would not have been so fastidious (as to devour a frail maiden).
159. "This has been a bad year for hemp."
160. ſieh.
161. a grotesque line!
162. Lieber Gott!
163. Cp. note 110.
164. einzig (not a misprint).
165. Note how the "dead" Piramus answers Thisbe with a line rhyming with her last.
166. A corruption of "Stanislaus" current in eastern parts of Germany at the time. Cp. note 131.
167. Cp. note 131.
168. In the following lines Gryphius ridicules the Reformation drama in which the moral was of paramount importance, and the form of little or no account. This kind of play lingered on into Gryph's own lifetime.
169. Another example of Squentz's 'erudition'. The reference is to the manner in which animals and even inanimate things converse in Aesop's fables.
170. narrates, talks.
171. The tale that follows is characteristic of the countless legends and fables appearing in the Reformation drama.
172. Squentz terminates his epilogue with a display of linguistic ability, viz.: a Greek word, a Greek word based on a Hebrew root, Latin and German.
173. The play is on the two meanings of „Sau": "sow" and "blunders."
174. A corruption of: regula de tribus numeris notis = Rule of Three. In Gryph's day it was still regarded as the finest achievement of medieval arithmetic.
175. Cp. note 99.
176. Adam Riese (1492–1559) was the most distinguished German arithmetician of the sixteenth century. His textbook *Rechenung auf der linihen und federn in zal, maß und gewicht auf allerley handierung* was first published in 1525. "Im ganzen deutschen Sprachgebiet wird wohl kein Name so oft in einer stehenden Formel gebraucht wie der des deutschen Rechenmeisters Adam Riese. 'Das macht nach Adam Riese soundsoviel' pflegen viele Leute zu sagen, wenn sie eine einfache rechnerische Operation vornehmen oder mit lächelnder Überlegenheit korrigieren."—Hans Sommer: *Kulturgeschichtliche Sprachbilder*, p. 83.

Johann Seckerwitz (Seccervitius) (c. 1520–1583) was by birth a Silesian. He acquired fame for his Latin poems and was appointed Professor of

Poetry in Greifswald in 1574. The association of Seckerwitz with arithmetic is probably meant to provoke another laugh at the confusion in the schoolmaster's mind. On the other hand, the appointment of "Professor of Mathematics and Poetics" was quite usual at the time.

SOME WORKS CONSULTED

Aikin-Sneath, B.	*Comedy in Germany in the first half of the eighteenth century*, 1936.
Alewyn, R.	Vom Geist des Barocktheaters (*Weltliteratur, Festgabe für Fritz Strich*, 1952).
Beare, M.	*Die Theorie der Komödie von Gottsched bis Jean Paul*, 1928.
Benjamin, W.	*Schriften*, Vol. I, 1955.
Bradbrook, M. C.	*The Growth and Structure of Elizabethan Comedy*, 1955.
Bredow, G. G.	*Nachgelassene Schriften*, ed. J. G. Kunisch, 1816.
Burg, F.	Über die Entwicklung des Peter Squentz-Stoffes bis Gryphius (*Zeitschrift für deutsches Altertum und deutsche Literatur*, Vol. xxv, 1881).
Chambers, E. K.	*The Medieval Stage*, 1903.
Coghill, N.	The Basis of Shakespearian Comedy (*Essays and Studies*, 1950).
Cohn, A.	*Shakespeare in Germany in the sixteenth and seventeenth centuries*, 1865.
Conrady, K. O.	Zu den deutschen Plautusübertragungen (*Euphorion*, Vol. XLVIII, 1954).
Creizenach, W.	*Geschichte des neueren Dramas*, Vols. I–IV, 1893–1909.
	Die Schauspiele der · englischen Komödianten (*Deutsche National-Literatur*, Vol. XXIII, no date).
Doran, M.	*Endeavors of Art*, 1954.
Flemming, W.	*Andreas Gryphius und die Bühne*, 1921.
	Die deutsche Barockkomödie, 1931 (*Deutsche Literatur, Reihe Barock*).
	Die Auffassung des Menschen im siebzehnten Jahrhundert (*Deutsche Vierteljahrsschrift*, Vol. VI, 1928).
	Deutsche Kultur im Zeitalter des Barock, 1937–1939 (*Handbuch der Kulturgeschichte*).
Flohr, O.	Geschichte des Knittelverses . . . (*Berliner Beiträge zur germanischen und romanischen Philologie, Germanische Abteilung*, I, 1893).
Fürstenau, M.	*Zur Geschichte der Musik und des Theaters am Hofe zu Dresden*, erster Teil, 1861.
Goedeke, K.	*Grundriß zur Geschichte der deutschen Dichtung*, Vols. II and III, 1886–1887.
Gottsched, J. C.	*Nöthiger Vorrath zur Geschichte der deutschen dramatischen Dichtkunst . . .*, 1757.
Gundolf, F.	*Andreas Gryphius*, 1927.
	Shakespeare und der deutsche Geist, achte Auflage, 1927.
Hankamer, P.	*Deutsche Gegenreformation und Deutsches Barock* (*Epochen der deutschen Literatur*, Vol. II, zweiter Teil, zweite Auflage, 1947).
Harsdörffer, G. P.	*Poetischer Trichter . . .*, zweiter Teil, 1648.
	Frauenzimmer Gesprechspiele . . ., 1643 et seq.
Herrick, M. T.	*Comic Theory in the sixteenth century*, 1950.

Herrmann, J.	*Über Andreas Gryphius* (Programm der städtischen Real-schule zu Leipzig vom Jahr 1851).
Hitzigrath, H.	*Andreas Gryphius als Lustspieldichter* (Programm des Gymnasiums zu Wittenberg, 1885).
Holl, K.	*Geschichte des deutschen Lustspiels*, 1923.
Keller, A.	*Die Schwaben in der Geschichte des Volkshumors*, 1907.
Koberstein-Bartsch	*Grundriß der National-Literatur*, Vol. II, 1872.
Kollewijn, R.	*Über die Quelle des Peter Squentz* (*Schnorrs Archiv für Literatur-Geschichte*, Vol. IX).
Kutscher, A.	*Die Commedia dell Arte und Deutschland* (*Die Schaubühne*, Vol. XLIII, 1955).
Manheimer, V.	*Gryphius Bibliographie* (*Euphorion*, Vol. XI, 1905).
Markwardt, B.	*Geschichte der deutschen Poetik*, Vol. I (*Grundriß der Germanischen Philologie*, 13, I, 1937).
Müller, G.	*Höfische Kultur der Barockzeit* (*Deutsche Vierteljahrsschrift*, Buchreihe XVII, 1929).
	Deutsche Dichtung der Renaissance und des Barocks (*Handbuch der Literaturwissenschaft*, 1930).
Reuling, C.	*Die Komische Figur in den wichtigsten deutschen Dramen bis zum Ende des XVII. Jahrhunderts*, 1890.
Rist, J.	*Die Aller Edelste Belustigung Kunst- und Tugendliebender Gemüther*, etc., 1666.
Rotth, A. C.	*Vorbereitung zur Deutschen Poesie*, etc., 1687 et seq.
Salditt, M.	*Hegels Shakespeare-Interpretation*, 1927.
Schaer, A.	*Drei deutsche Pyramus-Thisbe-Spiele* (1581–1607) (*Bibliothek des literarischen Vereins in Stuttgart*, Vol. CCLV, 1911).
	Die dramatischen Bearbeitungen der Pyramus-Thisbe-Sage, etc., 1909.
Schmidt, C. H.	*Nekrolog der vornehmsten deutschen Dichter*, Vol. I, 1785.
Schmidt, E.	*Aus dem Nachleben des Peter Squentz* (*Zeitschrift für deutsches Altertum und deutsche Literatur*, Vol. XXVI, 1882).
Seiler, F.	*Deutsche Sprichwörterkunde*, 1922.
Sommer, H.	*Kulturgeschichtliche Sprachbilder*, 1943.
Tieck, L.	*Deutsches Theater*, Vol. II, 1817.
	Critische Schriften, 1848–52.
Tittmann, J.	*Dramatische Dichtungen von Andreas Gryphius*, 1870.
	Die Schauspiele der englischen Komödianten in Deutschland (*Deutsche Dichter des 16. Jahrhunderts*, Vol. XIII, 1880).
Tropfke, J.	*Geschichte der Elementar-Mathematik*, Vols. I & II, 1902–3.
v. Waldeck, F. M.	*Der Peter Squentz von A. Gryphius—Eine Verspottung des Hans Sachs* (*Vierteljahrschrift für Literaturgeschichte*, Vol. I, 1888).
Wander, K. F. W.	*Deutsches Sprichwörter-Lexicon*, 1873.
v. Weilen, A.	*Aus dem Nachleben des Peter Squenz und des Faust-Spiels* (*Euphorion*, Vol. II, 1895).
Weinhold, K.	*Das Komische im altdeutschen Schauspiel* (*Jahrbuch für Literaturgeschichte*, ed. R. Gosche, Vol. I, 1865).
Wentzlaff-Eggebert, F. W.	*Bibliographie der Gryphius-Drucke in: Andreas Gryphius Lateinische und Deutsche Jugenddichtungen* (*Bibliothek des literarischen Vereins in Stuttgart*, Vol. CCLXXXVII, 1938).
Wysocki, L.	*Gryphius et la tragédie allemande au 17e siècle*, 1893.

ADDENDA

Hinck, W.

Gryphius und die italienische Komödie (Germanisch Romanische Monatsschrift, Vol. xLIV, 1963).

Lunding, E.

Assimilierung und Eigenschöpfung in den Lustspielen des Andreas Gryphius (*Stoffe, Formen, Strukturen, H. H. Borcherdt zum 75. Geburtstag*, 1962).

Mannack, E.

Andreas Gryphius' Lustspiele (*Euphorion*, Vol. LVIII, 1964).

Tisch, J. H.

Braggarts, Wooers, Foreign Tongues and Vanitas (*Journal of the Australasian Universities' Language and Literature Association*, Vol. xxi, 1964).